PROCRASTINATE
NOW

Rethinking *Time Management*

THE MORRIS CODE™
VOLUME I

NANCY MORRIS

Procrastinate Now
Copyright © 2016 by Nancy Morris

No part of this publication may be reproduced, distributed, or transmitted in any form or by any means, including photocopying, recording, or other electronic or mechanical methods, without the prior written permission of the author, except in the case of brief quotations embodied in critical reviews and certain other non-commercial uses permitted by copyright law.

Tellwell Talent
www.tellwell.ca

ISBN
978-1-77302-346-5 (Hardcover)
978-1-77302-347-2 (Paperback)
978-1-77302-345-8 (eBook)

DEDICATION

To Rosemary – my "sister", you spur me on to be the best "me" I can be.

To Laurel – my BFF, you keep me grounded.

To Jane and Susan – your friendship and encouragement made this book happen.

To my clients and colleagues – you are my inspiration.

To my husband, Jim, and my stepkids, Heather and Andrew – there simply are no words for the depth of gratitude and love I feel for you.

CONTENTS

Introduction to *The Morris Code*™ book series xi
Introduction to *Procrastinate Now* xv
How to use this book xvi

Section 1: Procrastinate Now   1

Procrastinate Now 3
Types of procrastination 4
Behavioural-avoidant procrastinator 5
Decisional procrastinator 6
What others say about how to stop procrastinating 7
A new look at procrastination 8
It's your smarts 9
Underlying reasons for procrastination 12
Why understanding this new perspective is so important ... 13
Improving metacognitive skill 14
The one strategy that has the biggest impact 15
In a nutshell 18
    Selected Bibliography 19

Section 2: Rethinking *Time Management*   25

The Key to Success 27
294 Steps 29
Next Thing 30
80/20 Rule 31

Dreaming ... 32
Effectiveness ... 33
Time Account ... 34
PMA ... 35
Pass the Popcorn ... 36
Chance ... 37
What Ford Knew ... 38
Who's Running Today? ... 39
Burning Grass ... 40
Got Two Minutes? ... 41
Practice Makes Perfect ... 42
Unfinished Business ... 43
Information Overload ... 44
Risk ... 45
Perfectionism Hurts ... 46
The Real Priorities ... 47
Learn How to Say "No" ... 48
50% Off, Every Day ... 49
What Ducks Lined Up? ... 50
Give Me Tension ... 51
13,000 Emails ... 53
The Myth of Time ... 54
When I Retire ... 56
The Big Cat ... 58
Thank You ... 59
Choose to Act ... 60
Bad Days ... 61
Between 1 and 7 ... 62
Going Around in Circles ... 63
Act As If ... 65
I Expect ... 66
Focus on You, Not Them ... 68

Don't Tell Me Why 69
Win and Lose 70
Halt 71
Hope Won't Help 72
Trust 73
Simply Does It 74
Especially Well 75
Shoulding on Yourself 76
How to Prioritize 77
Set Me Free 78
The Power of the Pause 80
The Systems Have It 81
Tick, Tick, Tick 82
Right and Wrong 83
Who's Your Neighbor? 84
One Thing 85
Do Something Not Urgent 86
Learned Helplessness 87
Roll the Dice 89
Using Time 90
The Power Hour 91
On Your Feet, Mister 92
Doing What You Know 93
How We Learn Skills 94
What's Your Excuse? 96
Occam's Razor 97
Pushing Paper 98
Taking Action 99
Concentration 100
What's 15 Minutes? 101
Bang The Drum! 102
Hot Potato 103

Fix the Roof	104
It All Adds Up	105
I Don't Know How	106
Heavy Have-to	107
In the Coffee Shop	109
The First Seven Minutes	110
EPS	111
Me in the Mirror	113
Addicted to Love	114
Work Isn't Work	115
Motivation in a Minute	116
What Season Are You In?	117
Quick Slow Quick	118
Now You See It …	119
Pass It On	120
My Dad	121
Multitasking	122
Watch It … or Not	123
What Inertia Really Means	124
Taking It Too Seriously	125
Stop Interrupting Me	126
Doing Your Best?	127
Go Debrief Yourself!	128
Your Source of Success	129
Are You Nuts?	130
Flippin' Email	132
Tips to Clear the Desk	133
Geronimo	135
Want More Discipline?	136
Just Focus on Three	137
Getting Organized	138
Without a Doubt	139

Itty Bitty Bits of Time	140
28 Days More?	141
I Like Work …	142
Playing Catch Up?	143
Don't Micromanage	144
Dish up the Brain Food	145
Want More?	146
Selected Bibliography	147
End note	169
About the author	171

INTRODUCTION TO *THE MORRIS CODE*™ BOOK SERIES

In the 25+ years I have been studying the science of psychology in the business world, certain obvious facts have emerged about how to create success in one's personal and professional life.

First, the word "success" is best defined by the person using it, and nobody else. Unfortunately, people have a tendency to listen to what others say the definition of success *should* be. This leads us to chase our tail, trying to achieve their success when ours is actually so much different. This also explains why some people struggle to follow the guidance of so-called gurus – it's *their* success, not our own.

Second, uncovering our definition of success can be difficult. Our inner voice is often drowned out by noise in our head. You know what I'm talking about – the noise that whispers in your ear that you're not capable, you should be doing something else, you aren't good enough, you're making mistakes, nothing ever goes right, someone will discover you don't know what you're doing and all the other BS that blocks you.

When you combine external noise with internal noise, it's no wonder you can't hear yourself think!

My fundamental belief is quite simple, and it is this – the depth of your self-awareness equals the breadth of your success, however you choose to define it. This holds true for life in general but also for different areas in your life. For example, your definition of success in a personal relationship is probably different than your definition of success in a business relationship. And the success you define for yourself in your 20's is very likely to be different in your 40's.

So the degree to which you know yourself is the degree to which you can create the opportunities and make the choices and decisions that will take you where you want to go. This premise is not new, but it flies in the face of many of the books, articles, videos, seminars, workshops, life and business coaches, and other resources that are out there. This isn't to say there is no value in these resources; but every great solution requires a problem and even if the problem doesn't really exist, you can bet that somebody will create it anyway!

The Morris Code™ book series helps you deepen your self-awareness. *The Morris Code*™ is a set of simple attitudes and actions I have learned over the years to be the most effective in helping someone define their own success. Understanding *The Morris Code*™ helps reduce that internal, unhelpful noise so that you can deepen your own self-awareness.

In a nutshell, *The Morris Code*™ is:

1. Use procrastination to your advantage by understanding what it truly is.
2. Pursue performance goals persistently and consistently.
3. Stop shoulding on yourself and others.
4. Have more want-to's in your day than have-to's.
5. Personify integrity – say what you mean and mean what you say.
6. Live in your sense of source, whatever that is.

This first book in the series explores procrastination from a new, science-based approach. Plus, there are dozens of ideas for increasing your productivity and work performance by rethinking "time management".

We tend to have a lot of internal conversations about our work and whether we think we are effectively contributing to a greater good. Our workplace is also the base for many social relationships. These factors play in to our self-esteem and confidence, making the workplace an ideal place to start in a journey of self-awareness.

INTRODUCTION TO PROCRASTINATE NOW

There is no such thing as "time management". In fact, those who say there is are doing a disservice to those of us who want to be more productive and effective at work.

It is not possible to manage time. It is what it is. There are 24 hours in every day, seven days in every week and 365 days in every year (except, of course, a leap year). Attempting to "manage" these facts is futile. It is far better to work with reality than against it.

So if you have picked up this book to learn a bunch of "time management" techniques, put it back down.

What you will learn, though, are some of the key elements of "choice and action management". Given that we cannot manage time, we must focus on what we can manage. And what we can manage are the choices we make and actions we take with the time we have.

Some people will say the difference between the phrases "time management" and "choice and action management" is just semantics. Well, semantics is about the meaning we attribute to the language we use. And in my world of psychology, that meaning drives our behavior. What we think becomes what we do. So changing the language can change the meaning, and changing the meaning often leads to changing the behavior. Sometimes the best and simplest place to start is with the words we use.

"Procrastination" is one of those words that has been given a very negative connotation. That connotation creates a lot of useless internal noise about who we think we are. Yet the science (you probably haven't heard of before) shows that procrastination is a gift you have, not a personality flaw or lack of discipline.

I don't want you to stop procrastinating. In fact, I want you to do more of it, and in Section 1 of this book, you'll find out exactly why. You'll learn the ways in which procrastinating is one of the most useful skills you have and you'll discover a unique action for maximizing it. As you understand the theory and implement the action, you'll automatically and naturally behave in a way that is more effective and productive, without reading dozens of books or spending thousands of dollars on coaches and gurus you really don't need.

In Section 2, you'll explore over 100 other science-based and common sense ways to rethink "time management" so you can make new choices and take new actions with the time you have. The section is a collection of short chapters that take just a couple of minutes to read. They come from the scripts of my internationally distributed audio program, *Simple Sound Solutions*, which has been sent to over 3 million people on six continents since 2006. Each chapter explores one specific attitude (idea) and a practical action you can take to increase productivity and work performance. In fact, you can take many of the actions as soon as you finish reading the chapter.

HOW TO USE THIS BOOK

Section 1 is a full chapter outlining the science behind the benefits of procrastination and how to maximize it to your advantage. I suggest you start there, as it explains fundamental principles that inform most of the rest of the book.

I recommend you simply open Section 2 every day on a random page. Read the short chapter and find ways to map the attitude into your day. Take the action suggested and see what effect it has. Just read one a day, or every other day.

SECTION 1
PROCRASTINATE NOW

PROCRASTINATE NOW

Every workday, you jump in the car or on the bus to start your commute to the office. As you travel along, you're probably planning the day's activities, and it might sound like this:

"I'll get that report finished today."
"Debbie asked me to do a favor for her, so I'll work on that too."
"Before lunch, I'll make those five phone calls."
"Damn, I have that meeting with the boss."
"Oh, and I'll get started on the Big Massive Deal."

Then that to-do list of 5, 10 or even 15 things barely has the surface scratched ... because you procrastinate about some or all of the tasks.

Many motivational speakers, coaches, and so-called gurus would have you believe that every time you procrastinate, you are self-sabotaging. I can understand why they say this. Everyone procrastinates, so that creates a big target market into which they can sell their goods and services.

But why is it that, even with all the different tools and techniques to stop procrastination, everyone still does it? Because the gurus are missing the mark. The scientific mark.

In the 25+ years I've been studying business psychology and working with organizations large and small, I have found that my clients' procrastination is one of the most important tools for creating success. Yes, you read that right – procrastination is a tool for creating success.

Far from being a personality flaw or bad habit, procrastination is something that anyone – from a high school student to a CEO – can use to actually reach goals and build empires. By the time you've finished reading this chapter, you'll understand why I say this. And you'll have a simple, easy-to-implement way of using procrastination for your benefit, too.

Before we get there, let's start with some facts.

TYPES OF PROCRASTINATION

Unfortunately, the word *procrastination* is often used incorrectly. For example, not wanting to wash the dishes in favor of watching a TV show is not procrastination, nor is it laziness. All day, every day, we have a myriad of choices. Sometimes we choose A and sometimes we choose B, without significance either way. The appropriate definition of procrastination is the behavior of delaying or postponing something that needs to be completed (i.e. putting things off) despite knowing it will have a negative consequence. Of course, if repeatedly putting off doing the dishes is going to get you in trouble with your partner, then that is procrastination. However, if it is just A versus B, then it is *preference*.

Procrastination is a widespread human condition, different for everyone, yet everyone procrastinates. Well-known researcher, Dr. Joseph Ferrari, identifies three basic types of procrastinator:

- Arousal type procrastinator – the last-minute person who thrives on the euphoric rush (thrill seeker).
- Behavioural-avoidant procrastinator – the person who avoids tasks through distraction and excuse.

- Decisional procrastinator – the person who cannot decide.

Although there are many arousal type procrastinators out there, the behavioural-avoidant and decisional procrastinator are the two most prevalent. According to Ferrari, it is the combination of these two types of procrastination that constitutes the majority of someone's delay in completing a task. Let's take a more detailed look at them.

BEHAVIOURAL-AVOIDANT PROCRASTINATOR

The behavioural-avoidant procrastinator has the tendency to delay the beginning or the completion of tasks. Avoidance behaviours are the things you do to distract yourself from the task at hand. Usually, you use avoidance behaviours when you perceive the task is going to be unpleasant (e.g. writing a business report or telling someone bad news). A whole host of emotions may surface as you consider the ramifications associated with this unpleasant task. Frequently the emotion is fear, which can encompass worry, anxiety and panic. By engaging in avoidance behaviours, you escape these uncomfortable feelings and experience psychological relief.

Some classic examples of avoidance behaviours at the office are:

- Taking long breaks
- Reorganizing your desk layout
- Browsing the internet
- Frequently phoning friends or family while at work
- Chatting with your colleagues
- Knowingly overscheduling yourself
- Extending 1-to-1 or group meetings unnecessarily

- Daydreaming[1]
- Overestimating your ability to do something
- Downplaying the importance of the task

Now, here's the funny thing about using avoidance behaviour as a strategy. Think about this for a moment – you put off doing the very thing that would lead you to accomplish your goal. You end up not achieving the goal (or perhaps achieving it late with a lot of challenges) and this impacts your self-esteem and confidence. Of course, this creates a vicious loop because your level of confidence impacts motivation to do tasks now and in future. So, avoiding things is a really bad strategy!

DECISIONAL PROCRASTINATOR

The decisional procrastinator is the person who puts off making a decision, especially when it comes to conflict or choice. If you are a chronic decisional procrastinator, you may be in danger of *optional paralysis*. You create so many choices, you feel unable to choose, and therefore do nothing.

Researchers cite that one reason for decisional procrastination could be low self-esteem and/or minimal self-awareness. Should you chronically be undecided, you may be creating situations that ensure you never test your abilities.

---

1   As an aside, research by Daniel Levinson of the University of Wisconsin-Madison, demonstrates that children who are regular daydreamers actually have better working memory (the ability to juggle multiple thoughts simultaneously) than their less dreamy counterparts. Working memory capacity has been positively correlated with reading comprehension, IQ scores, and in the ability to handle multiple complex thought processes all at once. Furthermore, it has been argued that daydreaming is beneficial because it acts as a type of rest for the brain. However, these potential benefits are controversial, and are subject to individual trait and personality differences, sometimes making daydreaming an avoidance behavior with potentially negative outcomes.

There are times when delaying a decision has benefit. Often, allowing a set period of time to mull something over so your brain can work it through generates a thoughtful and effective decision. In a way, it's like active daydreaming – letting your mind ponder for a while, but with some direction toward a solution. However, the key point is that the time allowed for mulling is set. If you repeatedly return to an as-yet-to-be-made decision and keep putting it off, that's procrastination, not thoughtful consideration of a problem.

WHAT OTHERS SAY ABOUT HOW TO STOP PROCRASTINATING

Row upon row of self-help books, particularly those written for professionals, dedicate pages and whole chapters to a myriad of ways to stop procrastinating. Entire books outline plans, schedules, and systems. Motivational speakers and business/life coaches have webinars, conference seminars, and full day workshops devoted entirely to ending procrastination. They suggest that procrastination can be overcome through performing some or all of the following:

- Connect to your fear. Allow yourself to feel your fears so you can address them.
- Reward and remind. Reward yourself for getting the task done; remind yourself of the consequences of not getting it done.
- Reframe. If the task isn't important to you, find a way to make it important.
- Reduce distractions. Seclude yourself and only take breaks when needed or as a reward for accomplishing smaller tasks.
- Break the task down. Take the complex task, break it down to its smallest elements, and then tackle each of those one at a time.

These are all good tips and many are mentioned in Section 2 of this book. No doubt you do some of these things already and probably get some success. But it doesn't last. You still procrastinate.

If these tactics were *all* that were needed, though, you would have done them by now and put an end to your procrastination. Not only would you say good-bye to your procrastination, you would also say good-bye to any fear of success or failure. There would be no more sense of helplessness in the face of complexity, no more lack of motivation, no more not knowing where or how to start, no more paralysis by analysis. All these would be gone, because you did a few activities. But that isn't what happens in the real world, is it?

It becomes clear, then, that something else must be going on because procrastination continues.[2]

A NEW LOOK AT PROCRASTINATION

Given that procrastination appears to be something that is not going to go away, what might happen if we take a completely different view of it? What if the reason why procrastination doesn't go away is because it's not supposed to?

What would happen to the way you approach your work, your goals, and your sense of achievement if you thought of your procrastination as a mark of intelligence rather than a sign of incompetence?

Just imagine what would happen to your motivation and confidence if every time you procrastinated, you said to yourself "wow, isn't this interesting" rather than "there is something wrong with me".

---

[2] To me, the continuity of procrastination is what actually makes it gold dust rather than a personal failing.

What if you viewed your procrastination as a mark of intelligence rather than a sign of incompetence?

Of all that has been written in the pop psychology world about procrastination, most of it has lacked the rigor that empirical research brings to the subject. Science is beginning to shine more light on what procrastination is, what it isn't and how it can be managed (note I didn't say "stopped"). Innovative techniques, including advances in brain scans, are helping to reveal the hidden anatomy of brain wiring, giving scientists a fresh understanding of how thoughts, emotions, and behaviors are formed. It's this new science that has led me to a new perspective of procrastination.

IT'S YOUR SMARTS

Procrastination is essentially your *sixth sense* putting the brakes on whatever it is you are doing so you can pause and reconsider. When you procrastinate, in whatever form you're doing it, the higher levels of your intelligence are telling you that something is not quite right for you. Just as a fever is a physical response to an underlying infection in your body, procrastination is a behavioral response to an underlying problem or concern your intelligence is picking up on.

Procrastination can be seen as the result of your higher level, but nonconscious[3], thinking center becoming stalled, confused, or simply cautious of something that doesn't fit into its current patterns

---

3 *"Nonconscious" is a term used to describe the mental processes that go on without your conscious awareness. It comprises two components – (a) the preconscious, which is information not being thought of at the moment but could be if primed by a reminder, and (b) the unconscious, which is all the mental processes that you will likely never have cognitive access to, such as what happens in your brain when you drive a car.*

or that has generated negative memories. Known as metacognition, this "thinking about thinking" helps you learn, remember, organize thoughts and behaviors, understand both simple and complex matters, and regulate knowledge. Cognition is what you consciously think – metacognition is what you nonconsciously think about that thinking. In fact, without metacognition, you wouldn't be able to do most of the aspects of your job. The interactions of this database of knowledge and skill generates what are known as metacognitive experiences. These are the judgments, concepts, ideas, and beliefs you form while performing an action. They are the more conscious product of the nonconscious processes of your brain. Sometimes they are positive and you spring confidently into action immediately. At other times, metacognitive experiences are more negative and other regions of your brain begin to kick in.

One of those other regions is the amygdala. The amygdala is comprised of two tiny bundles of neurons located deep in your brain on either side of center. It plays a big role in your emotions and decision-making. Perhaps you are familiar with the "fight or flight" response which occurs, for example, when you hear a loud sound behind you and have the urge to run away. This physiological reaction is linked to situations involving a threat to survival, and it's also implicated in the behavior of procrastination. Here's how it works. When you start to feel overwhelmed by an activity (e.g. something challenging), the amygdala induces this "fight or flight" emotional reaction. It does this to protect you from negative feelings such as panic, depression or self-doubt. When a threat is detected, (for example when you begin to panic about your report), the amygdala rushes adrenaline into your system. Adrenaline is known to dull the areas of the brain involved in planning and logical reasoning. So, for neurobiological reasons, you may end up being convinced that walking around the office to say good morning to everyone is a good idea even though your report is due at lunch.

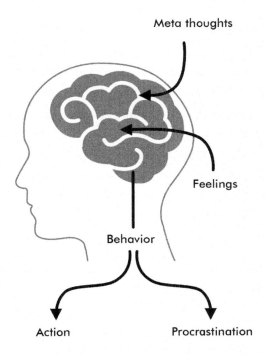

In summary, your higher levels of mental processing (metacognition) continuously generate metacognitive experiences – judgments, beliefs, etc. – about the task at hand. In nanoseconds, your brain weighs the positives and negatives to determine the next step. As this process unfolds through the amygdala, you will either start working on that report, or not. Either way, the thought and emotional processes of your brain evaluate a situation and determine what's going to happen next. You procrastinate when your brain is signaling that something is not quite right for you.

UNDERLYING REASONS FOR PROCRASTINATION

You sit at your desk with every intention of getting X done. As you reach for it, you pause and, *oh squirrel*, find something else to do. The "oh squirrel" is the behavior of procrastination. But it's not, in and of itself, a problem. It's a behavior. The problem is the mental processes (both conscious and nonconscious) that make you pause and notice the squirrel.

So what is the underlying concern or fear? When you have the self-awareness of what is going on underneath, you'll have the real reason and the real problem you need to resolve.

Most of the common reasons for procrastination fall into just a few categories:

- You feel the task has no relevance for you or it may be someone else's goal.
- The objective of the task, or the way it needs to be done, is unclear or confusing.
- The task is beyond your level of confidence.
- You do not respect, like, or trust the person who has given you the task.
- You think the process of doing the task will expose your conscious incompetence – in other words, reveal how little you really know.
- Similarly, the task creates a level of performance anxiety because you know someone somewhere will be judging your work or end product.
- You fear some type of physical, emotional, or spiritual harm will come to you.
- Doing the task goes against one of your core values and challenges who you are (e.g. selling something you feel isn't a good product).

When you procrastinate, your intelligence and nonconscious processes are putting on the brakes to say "hold on – something isn't right for me here." Instead of viewing procrastination as a hindrance to your success, embrace it as an important tool that can help you get where you want to go with confidence, effectiveness, and integrity[4].

WHY UNDERSTANDING THIS NEW PERSPECTIVE IS SO IMPORTANT

When you use procrastination as a pointer to your underlying mental processes, it becomes a mechanism for helping you develop self-awareness. Basically, self-awareness is an understanding of how you think and feel about yourself in different situations. Research shows that high-performing workers demonstrate high degrees of self-awareness and can more accurately assess their workplace behaviors such as procrastination.

The depth of your self-awareness is directly related to the breadth of your success, however you choose to define that success.

When you deny procrastination by seeing it as something to be "stopped", you are actually denying yourself that self-awareness. The more you focus on trying to stop the behavior of procrastination, the longer the underlying problem(s) will continue. You cannot fully stop the behavior of procrastination given that it's the behavioral result of high levels of thinking. However, you can change your thinking and set up new ways of dealing with the underlying problems.

---

[4] *While many people say they procrastinate because they "just don't want to do the task", most procrastination behavior at work falls into the eight categories mentioned. It isn't about preference. Not 'wanting' to do something is a convenient excuse for not wanting to be honest about the underlying problems or concerns.*

IMPROVING METACOGNITIVE SKILL

When you view procrastination as the behavioral result of your nonconscious (metacognitive) and conscious thinking processes, you open up a completely new way of creating success for yourself. Fortunately, research shows that metacognitive strategies can be learned. As your metacognition becomes sharper, the frequency of your "something is not quite right for me" decreases[5]. By improving your metacognitive skill, you gain confidence and become a more independent, focused worker. A quick internet search will bring up many articles and books that go into detailed descriptions for improving metacognitive skill. Generally speaking, though, metacognitive strategies include:

- Pre-planning – deciding what task to do and how to do it.
- Planning in action - modifying plans while you are doing the task.
- Directed attention – deciding in advance to work on the task.
- Selective attention – deciding in advance to remain focused.
- Self-questioning – asking yourself questions about progress, performance, and outcomes.
- Thinking aloud – verbalizing your actions for self-reflection.
- Self-evaluation – appraising your own performance against criteria or standards.
- Self-reinforcement – rewarding yourself for success.

---

5   While improving metacognitive skill does decrease the likelihood of procrastination, I cannot emphasize enough that procrastination does not stop, and you don't want it to. Each day brings new challenges, opportunities and tests of confidence. Procrastination allows you to learn and grow from all of them.

THE ONE STRATEGY THAT HAS THE BIGGEST IMPACT

As mentioned earlier, there are dozens of tips for managing some of the behavioral aspects of procrastination, many of which you will find in Section 2 of this book. While these are good resources, I have found a method that is by far the number one way to increase confidence, change thought processes, and reduce the problems that underlie the behavior of procrastination.

Fortunately, this method is simple and something you can implement right now. It costs nothing, needs no sophisticated software, and you can teach it to your family, friends, and colleagues so they too can create self-awareness and success for themselves.

This strategy can best be described by something Mark Twain said:

"Eat a live frog first thing in the morning and nothing worse will happen to you the rest of the day."

The "frog" is anything you purposely avoid doing and are procrastinating about[6]. It's the tasks that make you uncomfortable, particularly those that bring on conscious incompetence or performance anxiety.

By dedicating 15 minutes first thing in the morning to "eating a frog", you are dealing either directly or indirectly with the underlying problem that sparks procrastination. Plus, you are positively impacting both the conscious and nonconscious mind.

---

[6] *If you're avoiding a task because it goes against one or more of your core values, then you need to honor those values and "eating a frog" is not the right strategy to use.*

Think of your typical work day. You get up in the morning and, perhaps while brushing your teeth, you begin to think about that frustrating report sitting on your desk. You know the one – it's been there for two weeks. Here's what the conversation in your head may sound like as the day progresses:

"Okay, I'll start that report as soon as I get to the office. "

"After I've checked email and voicemail, I'll do the report."

"Oh look, here's an important email from the boss. I'd better deal with that first."

"Okay, it's 10:00 a.m. and I have all these phone calls I need to make. I'll do them now and at 11:00 a.m., I'll start on the report."

"Oh geez, some of those calls ran long. When I get back from lunch I'll start on the report."

"I'll just swing by Frank's desk on my way back from lunch and see how his project is coming along. Maybe he needs my help."

"Oh dear, it's getting close to 2:00 p.m. and I have a meeting. I'll try to do at least some of the report before the end of the day."

"Rats, I forgot that Client Bob asked for some information about X. I need to research it."

"Okay, it's 4:00 p.m. now. It's too late to start on the report. I'll get to that…as soon as I get to the office tomorrow."

Yes, you've dealt with the boss, the calls, and the client information. You helped Frank and went to a meeting. You probably got a bunch of other things done too. But all the while, the frog sat on your desk. And now it silently waves goodbye – again – as you leave the office.

Some of the underlying reasons for your procrastination stimulate the amygdala and generate degrees of fear, discomfort, and anxiety. One way of dealing with these negative emotions is by avoiding the stimulus that creates them (e.g. the report). As you can see by the internal conversations I listed previously, your highly creative brain can come up with all sorts of ways to help you avoid the stimulus! And it can do that for hours, days, weeks, and sometimes months.

You end up spending a lot of time in "avoidance" mode rather than "productive" mode. This also explains why you sometimes leave the office after a very busy day but still feel like you got little done. Instead of your highly creative brain being engaged in cognitively exciting projects and business solutions, it has spent its day avoiding a frog, and it knows it!

So after you eat that frog first thing in the morning, the power of your entire brain is available to focus on the real work at hand. Instead of looking for escape routes, you become more decisive, engaged, disciplined, and motivated. You see new opportunities and build a strong sense of confidence. Eating a frog for just 15 minutes first thing every morning[7] frees the mind for bigger things.

I often have new clients ask me to help them improve their performance and productivity, be more engaged, be a better manager, or develop other business skills. Rather than diving straight into strategies or plans, I simply ask them to eat a frog every day for one month. Sure, at first it can feel a bit strange, but within a couple of days, they get into the swing of it. Before leaving their office, they identify tomorrow's frog (i.e. task). By writing a description of the task on a note or placing the actual document in the center of their desk, it's ready to be devoured as soon as they get to work the next day. Some even place an actual plastic toy frog on the task as a reminder.

As various frogs die off, what appeared as the initial issue turns out to be a block created by an army of frogs that got in the way of my client's natural intelligence. By the end of the month, the original remit for our work has transformed into something completely different. Plus, as the client's self-awareness increases, the specifics

---

7   *If the task will take longer than 15 minutes, just eat a frog's leg. Break the task into a series of daily 15 minute chunks spread out over the course of the week.*

of the underlying problem and its authentic solution has become more obvious to them without intervention from me.

IN A NUTSHELL

You can't eliminate procrastination from your life, nor do you want to. Procrastination is a powerful and positive behavior because it signals that your higher levels of thinking have picked up on something that is not quite right for you. It can help you deepen self-awareness to deal with underlying problems and create the exact systems and solutions that will help you get things done.

Know that when you are procrastinating about a task, you are doing so for very important reasons. Acknowledge those reasons and implement "eating a frog" to create even more success for yourself.

Now, go pick out tomorrow morning's frog!

SELECTED BIBLIOGRAPHY

Bakker, A. B., & Daniels, K. (2013). *A day in the life of a happy worker*. New York, NY: Psychology Press

Bennett, S. (2014). *Get it done: From procrastination to creative genius in 15 minutes a day*. New World Library.

Beswik & Mann (1994). State orientation and procrastination. In J. Kuhl & J. Beckmann (Eds.), *Violation and Personality: Action Versus State Orientation* (pp. 391-396). Seattle, WA: Hogrefe & Huber

Blunt, M. Retrieved from http://www.meetmb.com/

Branden, N. (1994). *The six pillars of self-esteem*. New York, NY: Bantam.

Church, A. (1997). Managerial self-awareness in high-performing individuals in organizations. *Journal of Applied Psychology, 82(2)*, 281-292.

Davidson, R. J., & Begley, S. (2012). *The emotional life of your brain: How its unique patterns affect the way you think, feel, and live--and how you can change them.* New York, NY: Hudson Street Press.

Doidge, N. (2007). *The brain that changes itself.* New York, NY: Penguin Books

Effert & Ferrari (1989). Decisional procrastination: Examining personality correlates. *Journal of Social Behaviour and Personality, 4,* 151-156.

Efklides, A. (2009). The role of metacognitive experiences in the learning process. *Psicothema, 21,* 76-82. Retrieved from http://www.psicothema.com/pdf/3598.pdf

Fernie, B., & Spada, M. (2008). Metacognitions about procrastination: A preliminary investigation. *Behavioural and Cognitive Psychotherapy, 36,* 359–364

Fernie, B., Spada, M., Nikcevic, A., Georgiou, G., & Moneta, G. (2009). Metacognitive beliefs about procrastination: Development and concurrent validity of a self-report questionnaire. *Journal of Cognitive Psychology: An International Quarterly, 23(4),* 283-292.

Ferrari, J. (2000). Procrastination and attention: Factor analysis of attention deficit, boredomness, intelligence, self-esteem and task delay frequencies. *Journal of Social Behavior and Personality, 15,* 185-196.

Fisher, P., & Wells, A. (2009). *Metacognitive therapy.* London: Routledge Press.

Flavell, J. H. (1976). Metacognitive aspects of problem solving. In L. B. Resnick (Ed.), *The Nature of Intelligence* (pp. 231–236). Hillsdale, NJ: Lawrence Erlbaum Associates.

Flavell, J. H. (1979). Metacognition and cognitive monitoring: A new area of cognitive-developmental inquiry. *American Psychologist, 34,* 906–911.

Flavell, J. H. (1987). Speculations about the nature and development of metacognition. In F. E. Weinert & R. H. Kluwe (Eds.), *Metacognition, Motivation, and Understanding* (pp. 21–29). Hillside, NJ: Lawrence Erlbaum Associates.

Fleming, S. M. (2014). The power of reflection: Insight into our own thoughts, or metacognition, is key to higher achievement in all domains. *Scientific American Mind, 25(5),* 30-37. doi:10.1038/scientificamericanmind0914-30

Garner, R., & Alexander, P. A. (1989). Metacognition: Answered and unanswered questions. *Educational Psychologist, 24(2),* 143-158. doi:10.1207/s15326985ep2402_2

Hacker, D. J., Dunlosky, J., & Graesser, A. C. (2009). *Handbook of metacognition in education*. New York: Routledge.

Jaffe, E. (n.d.). Why wait? The science behind procrastination. *Association for Psychological Science*. Retrieved from http://www.psychologicalscience.org/index.php/ publications/observer/2013/april-13/why-wait-the-science-behind-procrastination.html

Levinson, D. J. (1986) A conception of adult development. *American Psychologist, 4*, 3–13. doi:10.1037/0003-066X.41.1.3.

Livingston, J. A. (1997). *Metacognition: An overview*. Retrieved from http://gse.buffalo.edu/fas/shuell/CEP564/Metacog.htm

Mitchell, J. R., Smith, J. B., Gustafsson, V., Davidsson, P., & Mitchell, R. K. (2005). Thinking about thinking about thinking: Exploring how entrepreneurial metacognition affects entrepreneurial expertise. Retrieved from https://www.researchgate.net/profile/Per_Davidsson/publication/27481727_Thinking_About_Thinking_About_Thinking_Exploring_how_Entrepreneurial_Metacognition_Affects_Entrepreneurial_Expertise/links/00463521551b2cf5b8000000.pdf

Morris, N. (2016). *Metacognitive skills training as a positive psychology intervention for within-person fluctuations of wellbeing at work* presented to University of East London, London, England.

Nietfeld, J. L., & Shraw, G. (2002). The effect of knowledge and strategy explanation on monitoring accuracy. *Journal of Educational Research, 95*, 131–142.

Orellana-Damacela, L. E., Tindale, R. S., & Suarez-Balcazar, Y. (2000). The impact of self-discrepancies on people's tendency to procrastinate. *Journal of Personality and Social Behavior, 15*, 225-238

Pinker, S. (1997). *How the mind works*. New York, NY: Norton.

Pinker, S. (2002). *The blank slate: The modern denial of human nature*. New York, NY: Viking.

Posner, M. I., & Snyder, C. R. R. (1975). Attention and cognitive control. In Solso, R. L. (Ed). *Information Processing and Cognition: The Loyola Symposium*. Hillsdale, NJ: Erlbaum Associates.

Pressley, M., Borkowski, J. G., & Schneider, W. (1987). Cognitive strategies: Good strategy users coordinate metacognition and knowledge. In R. Vasta, & G. Whitehurst (Eds.), *Annals of Child Development, 4*, 80–129. Greenwich, CT: JAI Press.

Rabin, L.A., J. Fogel and K.E. Nutter-Upham (2011). Academic procrastination in college students: The role of self-reported executive function. *Journal of Clinical and Experimental Neuropsychology 33.3*: 344-57. (Peer Reviewed Article)

Sabini, J., & Silver, M. (1982). *Moralities of everyday life*. New York: Oxford University Press.

Schraw, G. (1998). Promoting general metacognitive awareness. *Instructional Science, 26(1)*, 113-125. doi:10.1023/A:1003044231033

Schraw, G., & Dennison, R. S. (1994). Assessing metacognitive awareness. *Contemporary Educational Psychology, 19*, 460–475.

Self-awareness and metacognition. (2007, August 16) Retrieved from http://complexworld.pbworks.com/w/page/16266302/Self-awareness and metacognition

Showry, K., Mendemu, V. & Manasa, L. (2014). Self-awareness: Key to effective Leadership. *IUP Journal of Soft Skills, 8(1)*.

Tarricone, P. (2011). *The taxonomy of metacognition*. New York, NY: Psychology Press.

Wegner, D. & Giuliano, T. (1982). The forms of social awareness. In *Personality, Roles, and Social Behavior*. New York: Springer-Verlag. doi:10.1007/978-1-4613-9469-3_6

SECTION 2
RETHINKING *TIME MANAGEMENT*

This Section is a compilation of original, pre-edited scripts from the *Simple Sound Solutions* daily audio program that has already been sent to over 3 million people on six continents. Each script shares an attitude and action that will help you rethink "time management".

To get the most benefit from this Section, open it to a random page every day after "eating a frog" (explained in Section 1). Find ways to map the attitude into your day. Take the action suggested and see what effect it has for you.

Hint – listeners of the *Simple Sound Solutions* audio program tell me they enjoy sharing the attitude and action with other people. Not only does it deepen their own learning ("the best way to learn is to teach") but talking it over, debating and discussing the point helps the colleague, friend or family member, too.

THE KEY TO SUCCESS

Attitude – Many people ask me what the key to success really is. Well, I've decided that, right now, I will reveal all.

I'm going to tell you the answer. Ready? The key to success is … let's hear a drum roll … non-existent.

There is no one single key to success.

Geez, if there were, don't you think someone would have boxed it up and sold it for a gazillion dollars by now?

People advertise the big miracle maker, the best thing since sliced bread and the one program that you must buy today at this time-limited price that will give you a return on your investment of 10 billion percent.

Really? Wow, who-da-thought?!

Look, there is no *one thing*. Success in whatever we're doing is a combination of many things. I believe they fall into two main categories - what I call attitude and action.

"Attitude" represents the mindset of success and "action" represents the skillset. The great thing is that both can be learned, which makes it available to everyone.

Don't let yourself think that only hoity-toities with a big education and an even bigger wallet can create success. That is a lie some scared people tell you to keep you small and in your place.

Nothing stops you from creating what it is that you want, whether that is significant financial wealth or the abundance that comes from great relationships and healthy living.

Action – There are a lot of legitimate books, courses, programs, videos and more out there to help you further understand your attitudes and actions.

But if you don't want to invest in one or more of those, you only need to ask yourself these two questions.

First, *"do I have a mindset for success*?" In other words, are you positive, eager, determined and ready to commit to taking action? If yes, fabulous. If no, then that's a great place to start.

Second, *"what skills do I need to create the things I want?"* There's no right or wrong answer here. Just get a sense from yourself what might be missing and find ways to learn new skills.

———————————————

Success, in any endeavor, is actually quite simple.
Truly.
And it is waiting for you.

294 STEPS

Attitude – Watching toddlers learn how to walk is more than just endearing. There's a valuable lesson they teach us with their efforts.

You see, a toddler will take about 294 attempts to learn how to walk. That's right – 294. This shows us that we are actually born with what we need to create what we want. We are born with perseverance, desire and determination.

Toddlers don't give up. And if they did, you'd be reading this on the kitchen floor!

But as we get older, we try less and less. As adults, we often don't even try something simply because we *think* we might fail.

Somewhere along the line we learn to give up.

But that's not what kids do.

Action – Make a list of all those goals you dropped because a voice in your head said "I can't do this".

Then look at your list again with the eyes of a toddler who absolutely knows they can walk. And then take the next step.

You were born with perseverance. It's not something you need to learn how to do.

NEXT THING

Attitude – Feeling a little overwhelmed today and not sure what to do? Well, there really is only one thing you need to do.

The next thing. That's right. Just do the very next thing.

We feel overwhelmed by all the things we think we need to do. But many of those things actually can't be done now anyway.

Here's part of an actual writing project to-do list that my overwhelmed client, Frank, shared with me:
- Confirm objectives
- Gather all information
- Write an outline
- Speak to Bob about the outline
- Write first draft
- Gather draft images
- Write second draft
- Revise as needed
- Cross reference where appropriate
- Blah blah blah

And that's only one of his projects! Poor Frank was wasting time feeling overwhelmed by everything he saw on the list even though he hadn't even confirmed the objectives yet.

Action – Brainstorm all the tasks that need to get done on one of your projects. Then identify the *very next thing* and only focus on that. Only do that.

Keep doing the very next thing until you feel any overwhelm subside and the momentum return.

80/20 RULE

Attitude – Have you ever heard of the 80/20 rule? It states that 80% of your success comes from just 20% of your actions.

I have a different 80/20 rule of my own. It states - 80% of success comes from…getting started!

80% of the outcome of your goal, including work-related tasks and projects, is based on whether you actually start working towards it. And that's where people have the greatest struggle – getting started.

You may have all sorts of excuses for why you can't start toward a goal. It's the wrong day, you don't have the money, blah blah blah.

Just start. If it's something you really want to have, you'll find a way, even if you means getting other people to help you.

Action – What is that one goal, task or project you keep putting off? Start it today. Clarify the goal, plan the steps you need to take, and get started *today*.

Once you start, you're already 80% there.

DREAMING

Attitude – I used to get into trouble at school staring out the window. "Nancy, stop dreaming and get to work." Sound familiar?

Here's how to turn your dreaming into success.

But first, understand this – successful people are dreamers. Read the biography of most successful people and you'll see they have all spent time dreaming. Some even schedule time to stare out the window! (I'm not kidding!)

A dream is your vision of long-held desires and ambitions.

Unfortunately, we are often told not to dream. Or we tell ourselves "that's just a dream – it will never happen."

Yup, that's true. It will never happen … unless you do something with it!

Action – Take your dream out of your head and put it on paper using words, pictures or anything else that will help you see it in 3D. Put this vision board in a prominent place you'll see at least 4 times a day.

You'll soon be taking concrete steps to turn dreams into reality.

EFFECTIVENESS

Attitude – I get a lot of phone calls from people who want to know how to be more efficient at work. But I just don't understand why they want to know!

Being efficient is not the way to get promoted, make more money or achieve any of your goals. To achieve success you have to do something else.

You must be effective.

Being efficient is doing things right. Being effective is doing the right things (read that again).

You can be as efficient as you like doing things right. But if you aren't being effective by doing the right things, you're wasting time.

So what's the right thing? It's the thing that moves you forward.

Action – Today, ask yourself this: *Based on my objectives today, what is the most effective thing I can do right now?*

As you take more effective actions on a daily basis, you will naturally become more efficient too!

TIME ACCOUNT

Attitude - If I gave you $86,400, how would you spend it in the next 24 hours (how you answer that question is quite telling)?

Would your priorities be to pay off the mortgage or credit cards and feel more financially secure? Start a new business to feel independent? Or have a vacation to rejuvenate your soul?

Spending all that money on things important to you is really easy.

Why then do we often have trouble spending *time* on the *things* important to us? You receive 86,400 seconds every 24 hours. Yet I'll bet you don't spend much of it on the things you *really* want.

Rather, you allow yourself to be distracted by mundane things. Or things that frighten you. Or just plain old bad habits.

Action - Today, write out your top priorities and keep track of the time you *really* give to them. Be honest, clear and complete.

If you aren't prioritizing your time the same way you would prioritize your money, how do you expect to get what you want?

PMA

Attitude – PMA. Positive Mental Attitude. What a great phrase!

And you know what – some days the idea of a Positive Mental Attitude just totally sucks! Maybe today is that day for you?

You were late for work this morning and the boss is in a snarky mood. Then, you spilled coffee across that finally finished project.

So much for PMA.

Ah, but wait. There is a middle ground. I call it PGMA - Pretty Good Mental Attitude. It's like saying "considering all the rotten things that have happened to me today, the best thing I can muster is a *pretty good* mental attitude."

Action – Write "P G M A" on a lot of sticky notes. Put them on your phone, computer screen, even the car's sun visor.

Whenever you feel it's one of those days and you just won't get to PMA, shoot for PGMA.

Give yourself permission to be just 'pretty good' today.

PASS THE POPCORN

Attitude – Popcorn is a great snack at the movie theatre and it's also a fantastic way to get things done at the office. Yup, at the office.

I'm referring to a technique called *popcorning* that helps you blast away small tasks quickly, leaving you feeling productive and accomplished.

For this technique, you will need a small digital timer, often found in the grocery store or kitchen gadgets section of a dollar shop.

Action – Set the timer for, say, 10 minutes. As it counts down, stay focused on a single task, like filing or deleting old emails. When you hear the timer ring out, reset it for another 10 minutes and focus on a different task, such as organizing your desk. Keep doing this for a period of time, such as 30 or 60 minutes.

Here are some of the things I do with popcorning:
- 10 minutes sorting old emails
- 10 minutes organizing the desk
- 10 minutes researching a new client
- 10 minutes for short phone calls
- 10 minutes for filing
- 10 minutes for organizing online systems

Simply choose the task and the amount of time and then hit "start". When you're done, sit back and take a look at what you actually got done in such a short period of time.

Popcorning is a wonderful way to be focused, get things done and feel like you're making progress.

CHANCE

Attitude – "Destiny is not a matter of chance, it is a matter of choice." You may have heard this quote by William Jennings Bryan before, but are you actually doing anything with it?

Your destiny, your future, really *is* a matter of choice.

Truly successful people know they need to create their future by choice, not by waiting for some pie-in-the-sky chance to come along.

Many frustrated folks say things like "when I have a million dollars, then I'll be successful." Well, that is leaving everything to the – let's face it – miniscule chance you might have a million dollars land in your lap.

You *must* make the opportunities that you've been sitting around waiting for. You must go after what it is you want.

Action – Make one choice, right now, that will create your future. Then take the action within the next 30 minutes.

Don't worry about anything else.

Just start from where you are with what you have.

WHAT FORD KNEW

Attitude – The automobile mogul Henry Ford once said "if you think you can or think you can't, you are right".

Those words point out an important fact. Important, but not always obvious.

Yes, if you believe you can't do something, you probably won't be able to do it. But it actually goes *deeper* than that.

Because, in the first instance, you won't even bother *attempting* it if you think you can't do it.

You see, *you are what you believe yourself to be.* If you think you are logical, you will behave that way. If you think you are stupid, you will behave that way. And, when it comes to getting things done, if you believe you can get them done, you will begin to behave that way.

Belief drives behavior.

The positive belief will lead you to 'act as if' it were already so. And it will become so.

It doesn't matter if you are rich or poor, smart or simple, busy or bored, tall or short, magenta or purple. If you believe you can, you will. If you believe you can't, you won't. No other excuses matter.

Action – Do you believe you can achieve the success you define for yourself? Write down an honest *yes* or *no* answer to that question. And from that answer, simply plan your next step.

Remember, success is a state of mind. So the more you know your state of mind, the more success you can choose to achieve.

WHO'S RUNNING TODAY?

Attitude – Jim Rohn said "Either you run the day or the day runs you." Which is it for you?

In fact, either you run this *hour* or this hour runs you! Hey, even this minute! No matter how much time is left in your day when you read this, you can still make that choice.

If your "whole day" is going sour, then it is running you. And considering that the number of days we actually have is finite, how long do you want to keep this up?

A day can never really be a "write off", nor can your day be "wasted". In any given moment, you can change the direction of anything that is happening in your world.

Action – So today, this hour, this minute, what is your conscious choice? Stick a note on your computer, phone or desk with your answer.

_____

Are you running the show here or what?

BURNING GRASS

Attitude – When you were a kid, did you burn blades of grass with a magnifying glass? (I did) If you did, you were actually teaching yourself a fundamental key to success.
Focusing.
In other words, directing all your energy and effort to a finite, sharp point.
Just like the heat generated as the magnifying glass focused the sun's rays on the grass, you create success by bending all attention toward a work activity.
Whenever you concentrate with that level of intensity, you cannot help but get things done.
Focus, focus, and focus some more, and do not allow yourself to become distracted. Do not diffuse your own light by trying to put your attention on too many things at once.

Action – On a scale of 1 to 10 with 1 being "a complete nightmare" and 10 being "totally organized and efficient", rate the state of your desk, cubicle or office.
If it's 10, great – go celebrate! If it's anything less than that, what can you do *right now* to move it closer to 10 so that you eliminate some distractions? Do it!

The simple act of removing even one distraction makes being focused that much easier.

GOT TWO MINUTES?

Attitude – Sometimes, the height of the in-basket on your desk can feel quite daunting. And the more we put off doing the work, the more daunting it becomes.

Here's a quick technique I use whenever I need a boost of energy, a shot of confidence, or a sense of accomplishment for attacking that basket.

Action – Start by clearing a space on your desk that allows for two piles of paperwork.

Then turn off the phone and email system for no less than 30 minutes. If you can't actually turn them off, commit to not answering them.

Next, grab everything from the in-basket. Thinking about the very next action that needs to happen with each document or piece of paper, divide the stack into two piles - either "the next action takes less than two minutes" or "the next action takes more than two minutes".

Once the whole in-basket has been divided up, place the "more than two minutes" stack back into the basket. Then, do everything in the "less than two minutes" stack.

You'll be amazed by two things. First, just how much stuff has been hanging around for longer than necessary and, second, just how much you can get done in two minutes.

Sometimes, it's the little things that make the biggest difference (in many ways).

PRACTICE MAKES PERFECT

Attitude – They say practice makes perfect. So my question to you is – what are you perfecting?

Are you perfecting how to be effective and balanced? Or are you perfecting feeling stressed and overwhelmed?

Maybe you're perfecting putting your priorities first. Or perhaps you're perfecting how to be unfocused.

Are you disciplined and decisive or all over the place, unable to say "no" to others?

What you *continue* to practice you *continue* to perfect.

Action – Write down just two of your limiting habits. You know what they are!

Now write two habits you'd like to have. Don't just make them opposites to the limiting habits you wrote down. (You cannot just break habits, you must actually replace them with something different.)

For the next month, set goals and make plans to deal with just these four habits – the two you're getting rid of and the two you're implementing. Make this change happen.

Practice and perfect only those habits that
will take you to where you want to go!

UNFINISHED BUSINESS

Attitude – You have unfinished business that is holding you back. But I'm not referring to paperwork or projects. I'm talking about personal unfinished business between you and someone else.

If you're feeling angry or resentful, it's sapping your get-up-and-go. Even if those negative thoughts are in the back of your mind, they still take up time and energy.

Every grudge you hold equates to hours of ill-feeling, decreased motivation or just angry thoughts and behaviors.

Do something to take care of this unfinished business right now.

Action – Write a letter and either send it or burn it. Talk to the person directly and clear the air or agree to disagree. Or simply forgive and move on. You never have to see or speak to them again. And even if you do, you can still control your response by shifting your attitude.

Personal unfinished business can be far more destructive to your long-term productivity and success than incomplete projects or stacks of paper.

INFORMATION OVERLOAD

Attitude - Are you suffering from information overload? Feeling overwhelmed by having too much information coming in is actually caused by the illusion that we need more information!

Information management has many layers but one of the most important is to reduce the total amount that needs managing. In other words, stop looking for information you don't actually need.

I learned this lesson a few years ago one Monday afternoon while chatting with a colleague. I told her I needed to hang up the phone because there were tons of emails coming in. She had the same so-called problem, but as we briefly chatted about it, it became apparent that we had two different situations. My inbox was loaded with industry newsletters and broadcasts while hers was filling up with client questions and requests.

That day, I took my name off 75% of my email subscriptions. The inbox immediately became quieter (which ironically brought up odd feelings of not being a part of the action). I soon realized that the remaining subscriptions were more than enough to give me the information that I needed. Soon, my quiet inbox started filling again as more and more clients made contact.

Don't get me wrong - I love information. In fact, much of my business relies on my curious nature and access to new and timely information. But now, I'm very specific and choosy about where I get stuff.

Action - I challenge you to unsubscribe today (right now, in fact) from at least 25% of your electronic or print information sources. Determine what information is important, identify the most appropriate and trustworthy sources, and just get rid of the rest!

It's okay not to know everything that is going on.
In fact, in some ways, it is essential.

RISK

Attitude – If risk scares most of us, why do we ride rollercoasters?
Here's how the mind measures risk:
Imagine you're waiting to jump on a rollercoaster. As I go through this list below, decide when the ride has become too risky:
It has started to rain
The equipment looks old
Rusted bolts are lying on the ground
The ride operator looks drunk
The park was shut earlier with safety problems
The ride operator is definitely drunk
Everyone will answer differently and some will still be waiting for something more serious!
You see, risk is actually fear. And you aren't moving something forward because you're frightened by some factor or possible outcome.
But is any of it true? The way to handle fear is to challenge it.

Action – Write down a list of possible factors and outcomes that are frightening you. Work through the reality of each one with someone you trust. Challenge those fears!

If you don't take risks, you won't achieve success.

PERFECTIONISM HURTS

Attitude – Perfection gets in the way of getting things done. Plain and simple.

Perfection exists in a flower, or in the way the light dances on the lake at sunset or in the delicate and unique shape of a snowflake. Is it possible to create *that* kind of perfection in the email you are about to write?

No, but shooting for *excellence* in everything you do is definitely possible.

I'm sure you know people who are perfectionists – where everything has to be totally controlled and "just so". And no doubt they drive you ever so slightly nuts from time to time!

Many perfectionists actually struggle at work because they spend so much time dotting the very last *i* and crossing the last *t* that they don't get many other things done. It is a form of self-sabotage.

Action – Are you a perfectionist? If so, and you find yourself frustrated and bogged down with too much to do, try this exercise. (If you're not, teach this to someone who is.)

Every day, decide that one thing is completed even though, in your mind, it is only 90% perfect.

And then move on.

Actor Michael J. Fox nailed it when he said "I'm careful not to confuse excellence with perfection. Excellence I can reach for; perfection is God's business."

THE REAL PRIORITIES

Attitude – Tell me something…what are your priorities?
Work, family, money? How about reputation, giving back or integrity?
Why is it so important to know what your priorities are? Because you can change how you feel in the blink of an eye when you change what you view as important.

Action – Think of something you're feeling stressed about today. Maybe you're worried that X isn't getting done or that someone is going to let you down.
Has it got anything, *really*, to do with your priority of, say, a happy family? *Really?* If it does, fine. Do something about it, because only you can.
But if it doesn't, take a few moments right now to focus back on what, or who, is really important to you.

By keeping your attention and energy on what your priorities really are, instead of those fiddly bits that show up, you will quickly get rid of daily stressors and keep your work activities on track.

LEARN HOW TO SAY "NO"

Attitude – A client of mine asked "how do I learn how to say 'no' to people?" My answer? "Saying 'no' is not a skill to learn; it is a permission to give."

There isn't anyone out there who doesn't know how to say "no". You see, we tend to say "no" to ourselves all the time. So we actually have the skill.

We just don't give ourselves *permission* to say "no" to someone else.

We don't want to be rude, do we? And we really do like to be needed, don't we? So we say "yes" to outside demands on our time and energy.

Sooner or later, if not already, you will run out of those resources. Like it or not, they are not renewable. When the time is gone, it is gone. And while you might get some energy back, it will probably not be as powerful as before.

What is it going to take for you to give yourself permission to say "no" to someone's request of you?

Action – Today, in a situation where you would normally say "yes" to someone's request, choose to say "no".

Just once today. See what happens.

By respectfully saying "no" just once a day, your comfort level, and then permission level, will grow.

50% OFF, EVERY DAY

Attitude – If you follow the simple steps I'm about to share with you, you will cut the amount of time it takes to get things done by at least 50%.

In fact, I'm so confident in what I say that if these don't cut your work in half, I'll do your work myself!

Action – First, know exactly where you want to be by the end of the day. Keep your performance goal in mind.

Second, do not keep your schedule so tight with meetings and appointments that you have no flexibility for inevitable disruptions. For example, schedule just 6 hours of your 8 hour day.

Third, stay organized. Have certain piles or folders on your desk for certain types of work.

Fourth, make yourself accountable to someone that you like and respect, which isn't always the boss.

Fifth, do the thing you find most unpleasant first thing in the morning, every day.

Sixth, focus on just three things from your to-do list at any one time. Get those done and then move on to the next three.

And finally, celebrate all your achievement at the end of the day with a pat on your own back.

Rinse and repeat tomorrow.

Having a reliable, simple system every day cuts real and perceived workloads in half.

WHAT DUCKS LINED UP?

Attitude – The more negative words you use to describe your day, the more negative your day will be.

I often hear people complain about what has not worked, what doesn't fit and how things should be. They use up a lot of energy on being negative.

Well, let's have a look at the effect of that by doing a few calculations.

How many things had to go right in order for you to get through yesterday? What ducks had to line up in the right way for you to be able to get to work, attend those meetings, enjoy coffee with a friend, make the phone calls, and get home in one piece?

I'm not saying life doesn't have its hassles or challenges. I experience broken computers, busy signals, difficult people, and lineups at the gas station when I'm already late for a meeting. These things can be annoying, but why give them so much power that they cancel out all the positive things that happen to you every single day?

Action – Starting right now, begin jotting down all the positive things that happen today. It could be as simple as the computer turning on to something far more complex like that deal finally closing or that massive project being completed.

As you begin to focus on the things that go right in your life, what goes wrong will become insignificant.

GIVE ME TENSION

Attitude – Bridges are an amazing feat of architecture. Some are just a few feet long, going over a little stream. Others span huge distances, sometimes miles. Every bridge makes it possible for us to easily get from one location to another.

What's all this got to do with getting things done at work?

Well, the very thing that makes a bridge a bridge relates directly to our own lives. Plus, it can also explain why we often feel overwhelmed when we look at the stack of work on our desk.

Tension.

Think about this for a second. At exactly the same moment, two opposing forces are working on that bridge. One is the force of gravity, pulling it down. The other is the forces generated by the shape and structure of the bridge pushing it up, like its foundation posts or suspension wires.

These opposites work together to make that bridge stable. To make it something we can cross. If one force becomes stronger than the other, the bridge either explodes or collapses and we can go nowhere.

You may remember seeing pictures of the Tacoma Narrows Bridge collapse in 1940. That bridge swung and danced in the wind, for a variety of reasons. Bottom line, the construction of it was not appropriate for what is was supposed to do. Its *tension* became unbalanced. And it plummeted into the river with great style and fanfare (unfortunately killing a dog left in a car on the middle of the bridge).

Tension is what makes our lives work. Don't try to *reduce your tension*, unless of course it is extreme. What's more important is understanding how to *balance the tensions* in your life.

Action - Draw a line down the middle of a sheet of paper. On one side of the line, write out all the positive forces in your life. On the other, note all the negative forces.

Look closely - where are these out of balance with each other? Does one side have more things on it than the other? Are some quite extreme all on their own?

Put it on paper to see where you can take control of the opposing forces in your life.

Tension is good. Unbalanced tension is not.

13,000 EMAILS

Attitude – What would it be like to have 13,000 emails in your inbox? A business consultant I know has exactly that. And to him, it represents an easily searchable knowledge database and a quick reference tool for his ongoing work.

To me, even 10% of that number would be so overwhelming I wouldn't want to open my email system for fear of more coming in!

As I write this, I have 138 emails sitting in my inbox. Of those, 70% are new and the rest require some kind of action. Even though I receive over 250 emails a day, I can work them through and keep the number that sit in the inbox to a reasonable amount.

Action – Each of us uses our email system differently but are you truly comfortable with how you use yours?

To really know the answer to that, do you have any (and I mean *any*) negative thoughts or feelings when you look at the inbox or filtering system? If so, it is important to either redesign the system for your preferred outcomes or have someone else manage your account.

You see, the negative reactions we have to the seemingly positive techno tools we use significantly effects our day. Things that make you feel uncomfortable are getting in the way of your success.

THE MYTH OF TIME

Attitude – One of the biggest myths people believe in these days is that they can learn how to manage time better to improve their lives. Sorry folks – "time management" is an impossibility! The only thing we can manage is our choice of how we use the time we are given and the actions we choose to take.

Okay, you might be saying "that's just a semantics thing." That's not the case, though. It is actually a "mindset" thing. You cannot create more time, you cannot lose time, and you cannot manage time. Plain and simple.

The mind must shift from "time management" to "choice and action management."

What choices are you making for how you spend the time you have? We all have 60 seconds, 60 minutes, 24 hours, seven days a week, and so on. It might feel like a 10 day week or that the past hour has whizzed by in a second, but that's just illusion.

Action – To understand the choices you are making with your time, you must be more aware of what you are doing every day.

For the next two weeks, keep track of everything (yes, everything) you do between 7:00 am and 7:00 pm. If you work nights or rotating shifts, find a 12 hour block that would be best to monitor. Create a table or use your scheduling system to keep track of how you spend your time in 30 minute chunks.

At the end of the first week, briefly note any trends you are observing.

At the end of the second week, set aside one full hour to review what you have noticed for both weeks and, as honestly as you can, answer the following questions for yourself:-
- When am I most productive?
- When am I least productive?
- What do I do consistently each day?
- What tasks take a long time for me to complete?
- What tasks take a short time for me to complete?
- What do I do to avoid tasks?
- What do I enjoy doing?
- What choices do I make that serve me well?

- What choices do I make that no longer serve me well?

List five choices you are now going to make to positively impact your time.

This time tracking action step is one you may be familiar with. And it may take you a couple of attempts to do this for a full two weeks. Many people either "don't have time" or mysteriously "forget" to do it. Please don't let excuses get in your way.

Knowledge is power, particularly when it comes to choice and action management.

WHEN I RETIRE ...

Attitude – Bob was telling me that, because his retirement is at least 20 years away, he doesn't really pay much attention to it today. He thought putting a few dollars into a retirement fund was all he needed to do *now* to prepare for his future.

Au contraire, my friend.

Everything you do today contributes to your tomorrow, even if that is 20 or more years away. It's called the Law of Accumulation.

Yes, some of us find it difficult to cast our mind ahead that far, but taking *no* action right now leaves the desired outcome less likely to happen.

How do you want to spend your retirement? Traveling, volunteering, and socializing? Do you want to start what I call a "leisure career" – a job you simply do for the joy of it? Maybe you want to spend a chunk of your time mastering a hobby or writing a bestseller?

Bob wants to travel North America in a motorhome. He imagines that he and his wife will go up and down the highways, visiting family and friends. He'd also like to use that time to develop his hobby of taking landscape photos.

But Bob has never driven a motorhome. He has no idea what kind he'd like or need and hasn't even considered the real costs of that kind of lifestyle, which are changing all the time. He may be putting retirement money aside now, but he doesn't know if it is enough. He has no contingency plan either.

If Bob continues along the current path of inaction, he may well find himself just a few years shy of retirement without sufficient finances, knowledge or time to pull it all together. Even worse, he may actually miss an opportunity to switch to this lifestyle a few years sooner.

The Law of Accumulation works both ways – do nothing today, get nothing tomorrow. But do *something* today and you *will* create what it is you want, perhaps faster than imagined.

It can start with simply asking a few questions: What do you need to do now to make your own future happen? What points do you need to consider, what factors are involved, who else will contribute to it?

Action – Take just 30 minutes today to put a plan of action together. Then create a ritual of giving 30 minutes each month to your plan. Take actions, measure your results and then adjust your next actions.

Start creating your future right now.

THE BIG CAT

Attitude – Mohini was a white tiger who lived in the Washington Zoo in the 1960s. Amazingly, after so many years, this rare but beautiful creature still teaches us a lot about the mindset of success and productivity, even though this is a sad story.

Mohini's original cage was a 12' x 12' square. Just like most wild animals do when confined to a small space, Mohini would pace around this limited enclosure. The keepers realized the cat's distress and decided to create a beautiful new habitat for her to run around in.

With a lot of anticipation, the magnificent tiger was released into her large open space. But she cowered in the corner of the compound, pacing around a 12' x 12' area. She never ventured any further for the rest of her life.

What we seek in our lives is possible, but we can inadvertently spend years in old patterns of thought and behavior. We may want to be productive and successful, create wealth, feel authentic or simply express our own creativity. Yet, each day we think the same thoughts and take the same actions that keep our lives small.

The good news is that, unlike Mohini, you and I can learn new patterns.

Action – The first step is to become aware of what you are doing. Every day, write out one thought or behavior you have that you feel might be keeping you stuck or spinning your productivity wheels. At the end of two weeks, see what common themes are showing up. Then consciously plan your next steps.

There is no need to remain caged in limited thoughts or behaviors, particularly related to work.

THANK YOU

Attitude – Sometimes people say they don't have time to follow a particular strategy that I share. Well, this tip is so simple, it takes longer to explain it than to actually do it!

I believe the foundations of success are attitude and action. And the attitude of gratitude is one of the most important.

We are often so busy moving from one thing to another or wanting more more more that we forget about being grateful. And the easiest way to demonstrate gratitude is by sharing it with another person.

I'll bet that, like me, you have many people in your life that you are grateful for – parents, siblings, colleagues, guides and mentors, friends and partners. And there are others, like your local shop clerk, great dentist and happy bank teller.

When was the last time you simply took two seconds to look one of these people in the eye and say "thank you"? I mean *really* look at them with heartfelt appreciation?

Action – Today, and every day, stop what you're doing, look directly into someone's eyes and simply say a sincere "thank you" for how they are contributing to your life.

There is little room for negativity when gratitude abounds.

CHOOSE TO ACT

Attitude – When it comes to creating success in your life, factors like money, IQ and status mean nothing, zip, nada, nil. Success is not created by any of those things. Therefore, lacking any of them is no longer an excuse for you!

You see, it is continuous effort, not intelligence or fortune that brings you what you want. Just because you don't have a big savings account or a college diploma doesn't mean you have to stay small.

Common icons of success are people like Bill Gates, David Beckham, Thomas Edison and Mother Theresa. They are successful in different ways, but they all share a common denominator.

And it isn't education or money.

They all chose to act.

They set a direction, a purpose, and moved along the path. Daily steps, sometimes hourly actions, took them forward. Some steps were less effective than others, but because they *chose to act* and continue to act, they ultimately created their definitions of success.

Action – Any external block you perceive to be in your way can be overcome. Start by accepting and acknowledging with gratitude where you are now. Decide where you want to be. Wave your magic wand and dream big. Then, plan the steps and get started with your actions.

Remember, things don't get done because you have a degree, a big bank account or a certain IQ.
They get done because you choose to act!

BAD DAYS

Attitude – Some days nothing works in your favor.

You know what I mean – everyone's phone line is busy, the computer breaks down, people cancel appointments, you bump your knee on the desk. You feel flat and uninspired.

Yet there are other days where everything seems to flow. All your meetings are productive and on schedule, someone you've been chasing actually calls you, all the lights are green on the way home. You can't stop smiling and your energy is high.

What's the difference between the two days?

You are.

It is said that everything happening externally is simply a reflection of everything happening internally. This means the bad days are sending just as much of a message as the good days.

What message are you supposed to be hearing?

Action – Write out the details of a recent so-called bad day. Read over the various unpleasant events and how you might have impacted them. Look for common themes, like overcommitting your time. Maybe there are several different issues, such as trying to multi-task while feeling unsure or being distracted from priorities.

Understanding how you are creating the bad days means you are more able to consciously create the good ones!

BETWEEN 1 AND 7

Attitude – You have an "ideal number". That ideal number can help you be more productive, effective, efficient and accomplished.

How? Well, that simple little number can have a really big impact on your motivation to get things done.

You do not always need to go for the big deals or massive actions. Simply take consistent persistent actions over time to be productive and feel accomplished.

Action – Pick a number between 1 and 7.

Okay, let's say you picked 3.

What would happen if you made three more cold calls each day? That's more than 600 possible connections in a year. If only 5% of those extra 600 converted, how much would your revenue increase?

What if you contributed three new ideas to your teammates? What possibilities would you be helping to create?

And what if you spent three hours more each week with the kids? How would your relationships improve?

Or have three extra hours per month quietly enjoying your favorite hobby or pastime? Or three fewer hours working unnecessary overtime?

What if, just for the sake of it, you tried three new experiences this year? What opportunities might arise? What might you learn?

Small things can create big results.

GOING AROUND IN CIRCLES

Attitude – In his book *7 Habits of Highly Effective People*, Stephen Covey shared his thoughts about how we can influence our environment. He shared this through what he called the Circles of Concern and Influence.

Each one of us has a wide range of issues that take up our time and attention – health, family, career, problems at work, national matters and so on. All of these create our total Circle of Concern.

Within that circle, though, is another area - the Circle of Influence. This is the only place our personal power, and capacity to succeed, actually exists.

Here – let me show you what I mean.

Take a sheet of paper and draw two circles, one inside the other. Label the outer one the "Circle of Concern" and the inner one the "Circle of Influence".

The outer circle represents all those things, issues and events that you have no control over. You may think you do, but you do not (e.g. another person's choices, the boss's decision, the functionality of technology, and so on). The more attention you give to items that fall within this circle, the less energy you will have, the more frustrated and disappointed you will feel, and the more unhappy you will be.

The inner circle, the Circle of Influence, represents all those things, issues and events that you *can* affect some positive influence upon (for example, whether you choose one task instead of another, how you respond or react to something or someone, your contingency plans, and so on). It is within this circle that personal power exists, potential evolves and your self-confidence grows exponentially.

Here is a simple yet typical example of how understanding this concept can work for your productivity. Let's say something at work is not unfolding as you would like it to. One of your projects is behind schedule and you're agitated. You spend time complaining to your colleague, John, that Bill has not been returning your calls and that Mark does his work too slowly. Resource deliveries are constantly late and you are worried that the whole situation is going to reflect badly on your reputation. You are clearly within a Circle of Concern.

Now it's time to turn on your Circle of Influence. What's working? What's not quite right yet? Who can contribute to the project's success?

Is there someone else who can make contact with Bill? How can you support Mark in his job performance? What information, resources or guidance does he need? Can you give those to him or can someone else? Do you see ways in which systems can be more efficient? What information or guidance do you need to find? How can this situation be improved? What are you learning?

Did you notice something there? Whenever we are in a Circle of Concern mentality, we are "making statements" – Bill never calls, Mark is slow, deliveries are late. And then we stop. We make statements and then … nothing. Nada. Zip.

Action – To shift into a Circle of Influence, start asking questions, of yourself and others. Who, What, Where, When, How. And then take action on the answers.

By moving from your Circle of Concern to your Circle of Influence using powerful questions, you are able to create positive energy and momentum that changes you and eventually influences others around you.

ACT AS IF

Attitude – Feeling a lack of confidence today? If so, there are three little words you can use *whenever* you feel unsure.
Act as if.
That's it. That's all.
Let's say you have to make a phone call that you really don't want to make. Maybe it's a cold call, or some other kind of call to someone you don't know. You're feeling hesitant. Okay, you're downright anxious about it.
Here's the scenario that may be playing in your head as you dance around the phone: "This guy doesn't want to hear from me. What if he is annoyed I'm calling? I don't really know what I'm talking about. He could ask me questions I can't answer and I'll look like an idiot. This is so boring. Why do I have to do this?"
You may wander away from your phone, hiding near the watercooler or suddenly remembering some old paperwork that needs your attention. Even an appointment with the dentist would be less painful than picking up that phone!

Action – Consider how someone who feels completely confident at the task would respond. What would he or she be thinking? How would they actually behave? What steps or systems might they have in place? How would they manage themselves in this situation?
Even more powerful is remembering your own attitudes and actions when you have been successful at something similar in the past. What did you do? How did you think?

Imagine, just for a moment, what you could create in your life if you simply acted as if you already had.

I EXPECT

Attitude – In my research, I've found that one of the most dangerous yet common phrases at the office is "I expected". Having expectations of how others should or should not perform is going to damage, if not destroy, your own success.

This is a controversial statement for me to make. Lots of motivational speakers or business coaches will say that if you passionately expect something to happen, it will, and that's a good thing. Well, it only works if you don't involve others in that expectation.

Let me give you some examples of the damaging work-related expectations I'm referring to:

- Expecting others to know exactly what and when you want something done.
- Expecting someone to respond in a certain way just because you did something.
- Expecting the guy down the hall to stop talking to you that way.
- Expecting the boss to reward your efforts in the way you want, when you want.
- Expecting others to have the same work ethic or method that you do.

Expectations are actually promises not yet communicated or agreed. I would imagine that most of your expectations are one-sided conversations ... with yourself. You've not told the other person what you need or want so how can they actually know? It's time to speak up and make some agreements with others.

Action – Today, when you are wanting something to happen, make sure the other person understands your requests.

If they agree, then it is a promise that can be managed. If they do not, then you are not left to expect anything.

From now on, whenever you hear yourself use the words "I expect", check to see whether you've been talking to yourself again!

FOCUS ON YOU, NOT THEM

Attitude - What's been going wrong at the office these days? What problems have reared their ugly heads for you?

Maybe the technology team hasn't resolved the glitch with your PC. Perhaps morale is really low and it feels like no one is taking responsibility. Maybe you feel like management simply doesn't appreciate all your hard work. Or one of your colleagues is just annoying the heck out of you!

I know - it's not always easy to deal with these situations. And they distract you from what you want to accomplish, right?

To solve any problems at work, the most productive focus of your attention is not on what others have or have not done for you but on what you have or have not done for *yourself*.

Where have you let your own standards of behavior slide? When was the last time you had a relaxing lunch? Do you need to learn how to say *No* to those who ask too much of your time? Do your colleagues really know what your boundaries are?

Action - Today, list five attitudes or actions *you* have that need upgrading or evolution. Then start working on the first one.

Focus your attention on what you can do for yourself and stop getting all wound up by what others are or are not doing. Let them get on with their own stuff.

DON'T TELL ME WHY

Attitude - In psychological terms, there are many phrases and words that impact your levels of motivation, persistence, productivity and enthusiasm. The one I want to share with you today is the word "why".

This is one of the shortest yet most destructive words we could possibly use. As kids, we used the "why" question to help us make sense of the world. As adults though, "why" often begins a question that invariably causes us to remember bad situations or go on the defensive.

"Why did you do that?"
"Why doesn't it work the way I want it to?"
"Why should they get all the glory?"
"Why can't I do this better?"

Just like an internet search engine, our mind will look for the answer to any question we ask of it. When our questions are framed in the negative, as most "why" questions are, our mind will usually uncover a negative answer.

"Why can't I do this better? Because I don't have the intelligence. Because I fail at this stuff all the time. Because I'm a dweeb."

While you may not consciously respond so pessimistically all the time, "why" often generates a negative response at some level.

Action - Start your questions in a way that encourages the brain to find a solution rather than an excuse or reason. Begin questions, either to yourself or to others, with the words *when*, *what* or *how*. "When can I commit to finalizing this? What three things can we alter to improve the performance? How many people are needed to implement the new plan?"

To get things done, start as you mean to go on
- with powerful solutions and motivation.

WIN AND LOSE

Attitude – Reframing is the art of changing your perspective or attitude in a way that motivates you to take another step. I'm wondering – how could you reframe "win and lose"?

Do you like to win? If so, you need to know that the need to win actually blocks productivity.

If we borrow from the science of physics for a moment, we'll see that for every action there is an equal and opposite reaction. Well, the same holds true for attitudes and opinions. When you win, you feel great and say wonderful things about yourself. But when you lose, it is likely that your internal language is harsh and negative. And if it is, then when you do win, you've not been motivated by a positive driver. You've simply been motivated to avoid the nasty internal language that comes with a previous loss.

Jack was perceived as being highly successful. He landed all the business deals, seemed to have healthy relationships and appeared happy. Yet he wasn't. He was so motivated *not to lose* that he couldn't enjoy his wins.

Jack could never appreciate what he had achieved because he was only driven by the need to avoid negatives. This strategy worked, but eventually avoiding negatives was burning him out.

And Jack is not an extreme case. Far from it actually.

But when Jack reframed *win and lose* into simply *pursuing his personal best with integrity*, he was able to relax and enjoy his life's accomplishments. Not surprisingly, he became even more productive and successful!

Action – Take something you need to win at, like a business deal, a game of golf, or out-gossiping the next guy. Reframe your position into something less black and white ... less win or lose.

The language we use influences our actions. Speak wisely.

HALT

Attitude – There are some great acronyms. For example, SCUBA means "self-contained underwater breathing apparatus", radar stands for "radio detecting and ranging" and the word laser equals "light amplification by stimulated emission of radiation."

One acronym I find absolutely ideal for a tough day at the office is HALT.

Taken from the many 12-step programs, HALT stands for hungry, angry, lonely, and tired.

These four factors are major contributors to that feeling of overwhelm at the office. Using HALT gives us a quick way to find solutions for our high stress and low productivity.

Action – Next time you feel agitated, grumpy or perplexed, ask yourself "am I hungry, angry, lonely or tired?"

If you're hungry, eat something, preferably protein.

If you're angry, figure out why and with whom.

If you feel lonely, call a friend or confidante.

And of course if you're tired, take a break.

Sometimes, you'll answer "yes" to more than one of the questions, so recognize what it is and immediately take action. If you're still stressed afterwards, at least you'll be in a much better position to handle what's really bothering you.

HALT yourself from time to time.

HOPE WON'T HELP

Attitude – Hope is a wonderful thing. When we "hope", we have a general feeling that some desire will be fulfilled. And hope often gives us energy in times of gloom or when we are casting our mind forward.

But whenever I hear someone say "I hope I get this project done" or "this quarter's sales figures will hopefully be better", I only have one response.

Hope lives in your heart, not in your work!

The phrase "I hope" loosely tossed into business-related sentences is a sure-fire way of signaling to someone, including yourself, that you really have no clue about what is going on or no real conviction to make something happen.

"I hope" tells me you are unsure, non-committal and probably not interested anyway.

And that is the complete opposite of success.

Action – It can be challenging to change the habit of using a destructive phrase like "I hope". Get the support from someone you trust to give you a little prod whenever you say "I hope" in relation to work.

Get support from others to signal your "I hopes" at work and leave the real hope to other parts of your life.

TRUST

Attitude – Trust. Often a very fragile thing. And despite how much we say we do or do not trust others, it actually has nothing to do with them.

Your ability to trust someone else is a direct reflection of whether you trust yourself. Trusting in others is a mirror of you.

Successful people trust themselves to manage situations regardless of what others do. They know they are capable of rising above the negative behaviors people have because they know they can't control other people anyway.

Successful people acknowledge human mistakes and move beyond the limitations of holding others to perfect behavior.

They build this trust by focusing on making and keeping promises to *themselves*.

Action – Every time you break a promise to yourself, you lose your own trust. The more often you let yourself down, the more you feel others do that, too. So you end up losing trust in yourself *and* in others around you.

You've got to walk your talk. If you say it, do it. Build your personal integrity, stop the little white lies, the broken promises and excuses.

Hold yourself higher, live your principles and learn to trust all that you say and do.

SIMPLY DOES IT

Attitude – Being productive is actually quite simple. It is we who make it complicated.

Over the years, and for all sorts of reasons, we learn how to complicate most things we come into contact with, including work tasks.

But we don't start off that way. As kids, we are actually drawn to simplicity. And you were probably more interested in the box the present came in than the present itself!

As an adult, anything that seems hard or complex to you has probably been created that way – *by you*. You can undo that learning by dividing any complex issue or task into very simple parts. As you learn to master the smaller, simpler bits, no task will ever be too difficult.

Action – What project, system or issue are you working on, or avoiding, that feels too complicated? List all the simple parts that make up the complexity.

———————————————

Master each aspect of your tasks, simply.

ESPECIALLY WELL

Attitude – I was speaking with a sales director at a large US company recently. Jennifer enjoyed her work but was increasingly frustrated that her longer hours were not yielding bigger returns.

I asked her just one thing. "Tell me all the things you do especially well."

Jennifer started, listing off all the things that she was doing at work, but that is not what I had asked her to do.

It quickly became apparent to both of us that, through a combination of corporate downsizing, higher organizational demands, and her own choices, she was doing a lot of stuff that she actually didn't execute very well.

And by taking on all these additional tasks – some would say they were requirements of her job – Jennifer found herself avoiding things, re-doing projects, feeling doubt in her ability, and generally fearful of what was happening now and next.

Some people reading this might say "I only do the stuff I enjoy". If that's true, great. But if you are working longer or harder with no significant return of money or enjoyment, this story directly relates to you!

Action – Write out two lists – one for the things you know you do especially well and the other list for the actual things you do in relation to your work. How big is the mismatch?

Doing things especially well, rather than just doing them, will help you feel and be more productive and effective.

SHOULDING ON YOURSELF

Attitude - Are you shoulding on yourself?
The word "should" is one of the most negative words in the English language. "Should" expresses a feeling of unwanted duty or misplaced obligation. But who created those responsibilities?
Here's how we make the word "should" detrimental to our success:
"I should do this better."
"You should do what I say."
"We shouldn't have voted him in."
"They shouldn't expect more than this."
I have yet to find an instance where "should" creates positive action. Sure, people might respond to shoulds, but it's a fear-based reaction.
Saying "should" about others is bad enough, but shoulding on yourself is downright destructive! How often do you should on yourself each day, particularly about work tasks? How do you normally respond to your own shoulds?

Action - Make a list of all the shoulds in your life. Today, commit to removing at least one of those, permanently.

Should less, choose more.

HOW TO PRIORITIZE

Attitude – With the average professional having 59 hours of work on their desk at any one time, how can anyone get it all done?

The answer is simple. You can't. What you *can* do is make different choices about what you do and when.

I'm often asked "Nancy, how do I balance my schedule?"

Simple. Schedule your priorities, don't prioritize your schedule.

The activities that are most important to your success are scheduled *first*. These are the actions and habits that will contribute the most to your goals and your top priorities. Everything else fits around these. And your top priorities don't get bumped. Period.

A salesman, Steve, realized that one of his priorities was his health. He knew that working out helped him be more effective and productive, yet he rarely did it. So he scheduled two morning timeslots during the week to go to the gym.

But what if a client wanted to see him at that time? He told them he had another commitment and they simply arranged another time. No client ever left him because of it.

And I'll bet you know the next part. Yup, Steve's productivity shot up and so did his commission checks!

Action – Today, review your schedule for the next two weeks. Are all your top priorities already written down? *In cement?*

Schedule your priorities first instead of prioritizing your schedule and you will immediately see positive results.

SET ME FREE

Attitude – Underneath the fancy car, big house, and hefty bank account, most people will confess that what they really want is more freedom to choose. Let me show you how you can make that happen in the very next hour.

Making choices is a decision. It is a permission you give yourself, or not, in any given moment. Even choosing not to do something is a choice. I know you know that, but are you actually living it?

The status, money and security you seek will not give you the ability to have more choice. The *content* of the choices may change but whether you have $10,000 or $10 million, it will not change your capacity to choose between A or B or C.

You have that skill right now. And not only understanding this but actually living in choice, starting today, will make all the other dreams easier to fulfill.

Action – For the next hour, write a list of all the choices you make. You may find this challenging because in 60 minutes, you actually make dozens of choices.

Here's what it might look like:
- I chose to do this exercise
- I chose to answer the phone
- I chose to speak to Bob for 5 minutes
- I chose not to tell him how the project was really progressing
- I chose to send two emails
- I chose to get coffee instead of starting that letter
- I chose to feel annoyed at writing down all my choices!
- I chose to change to black ink instead of blue
- I chose not to tell Frank about his ugly tie
- I chose not to call my spouse
- And so on

Don't judge your choices, just notice them.

_____

You choose everything you create and every task you complete. By acknowledging choice from now on, you will choose to create many amazing things.

THE POWER OF THE PAUSE

Attitude – For years, psychologists have known that taking short pauses throughout the day is a powerful way to recharge. These are what we call "mental health moments" and are essential for highly productive days.

Yet, few people actually use this simple and effective tool as a way to refresh.

We waste time looking for technology or techniques to help us refocus. Instead, all we need to do is ... nothing.

Pausing in your physical and mental activities for as little as one minute every hour is all it takes. You see, that mental health moment will drop your heart rate, redirect blood flow in the brain, relax muscles and calm hectic internal chatter.

Action – Set your watch or computer alarm for 60 minutes. When it beeps, pause all your activities – except driving – and take in 10 deep breaths.

Stop thinking or doing or acting for just one minute every hour and you will be see instant results.

THE SYSTEMS HAVE IT

Attitude - Having studied neural networks and the functions of the brain, I clearly understand the importance of systems.

Everything exists within a system. Our planet is in a star system. Your office is a system with hierarchies, structures and a culture all its own. And you are a collection of systems - physical, mental and spiritual.

So, seeing your to-do list in the context of a system will help you achieve your goals.

I was amazed at the simplicity of a question I heard a few years back (noted below). This one question allowed me to fundamentally improve my business results immediately by focusing on systems.

Action - Next time something isn't working the way you want it to, ask yourself this: *What system is missing from my work structure that is allowing this to happen?*

Maybe your to-do list is always having more added to it rather than subtracted. What system is missing?

Maybe you're touching tasks three or four or five times before actually working on them. What system is missing?

Even in your personal life, this question can help you refocus and plan ahead. *What system is missing from my social life that is allowing this to happen?*

Personal power lies in your ability to recognize your desired outcome, devise the plan and take the actions to make it happen. That is a system of success.

TICK, TICK, TICK

Attitude – Are you running out of time?

The lack of something, including time, is never the problem. It is the *symptom* of the problem. So what is causing the symptom of a lack of time?

Several things could contribute to feeling like there's no time, but usually it is a basic problem of priorities. Most of us spend lots of time doing things, but are those activities truly connected to your priorities, or are they just things to do?

I know I can certainly fill up my days with stuff if I choose to!

You cannot set priorities for your attitudes and actions without first knowing your personal and professional goals.

Action – What are your top three goals this week? What actions must you take to achieve those goals? And are you persistently, consistently taking those actions?

Set your goals, determine your priorities and then focus your time on making them happen.

RIGHT AND WRONG

Attitude – "I want to know I'm making the right decision." That is one of the most common phrases I hear in my work.

What makes any decision "right"? At work, many would say a right decision means someone gains some kind of benefit. Or that it means the best outcome is achieved. Or that it makes us happier or the company wealthier.

However, being right or wrong is simply a judgment. What is right for you may be wrong for me and vice versa. And right is a judgment that is only ever measurable *after* something has happened. So how can you expect to be right beforehand?

There really is no true right or wrong. These are simply words that live at either end of a spectrum. And it's entirely up to you what that spectrum actually looks like. Each person's spectrum is different.

I'm not talking about moral judgments here. I'm referring to the way we use "right" and "wrong" when we make decisions about our tasks and careers. It has taken me some conscious effort to remove the right and wrong spectrum from my decision-making process at the office. I now use different criteria based on my performance goals and desired outcomes to make up my mind. And I have taught many others how to do it too.

Action – Consciously make decisions that are based on information you have on hand right now.

Start by saying to yourself "based on what I know now, I decide X". Take this perspective as a first step to removing "right" and "wrong".

Don't worry about factors as yet unknown or elements that you cannot control.

WHO'S YOUR NEIGHBOR?

Attitude - We all live in a neighborhood. For some, the nearest neighbor is miles across a country field. For others, they are right next door. Either way, they are neighbors. Our neighborhood is extremely important to the way we perceive our world.

For now, let's look at our work neighborhood.

Do you like your neighbor? Is one of your neighbors a bully or a confidante? Do you enjoy seeing them as they go about their daily business or would you prefer they kept out of your way? If you could surround yourself at work with your BFF office neighbor(s), who would it be?

Action - You spend hours in your work neighborhood each week so it's important to put some emphasis on how this environment feeds you. Appreciate the neighbors who inspire you and avoid those who do not.

If there are many more people to avoid than not, perhaps it's time to consider moving to a new neighborhood!

ONE THING

Attitude – Winston Churchill said "continuous effort – not strength or intelligence – is the key to unlocking our potential."

Persistent, consistent action over time is the only way to achieve lasting success, at work and at home.

As Mr. Churchill said, it is not about strength. Being strong is not as significant as being boldly persistent, despite temptations to stop.

Intelligence is important but brains get you nowhere if you cannot consistently stay focused on the actions that will bring about your desired outcome.

And patience to stay the course over time – a characteristic Mr. Churchill had in buckets.

Action – Not sure how to be persistent and consistent over time?

Here's how. Every day this week, do one thing – just one – that will make a particular work goal more likely to happen. You don't have to achieve the goal this week, but just take the action every single day for the whole week. It could be reviewing your task list every morning before jumping in to the emails, or making five cold calls each day, or taking ten minutes to completely tidy the desk before leaving for home.

Just commit to doing one thing, and then do it every day. It can be that simple.

DO SOMETHING NOT URGENT

Attitude – Doing feared things first (i.e. eating a frog) is one of the best ways to lighten your day, build confidence and get things done. And now I'm going to inject another aspect into that best practice.

After you've done a feared thing first, do an important but non-urgent thing next.

Before you even open up your email inbox or begin making phone calls, set aside 15 minutes each morning to do something that specifically relates to a longer term project. You may choose to draft part of next month's project plan, or read one chapter in a useful book that is gathering dust on your desk. I will often do some of the administrative tasks needed to put my next book together or use the time to learn part of the software package that will manage my growing list of clients.

These important but non-urgent projects impact business in significant ways. But once we get into the day's activities that usually involve other people or tight deadlines, we forget all about our longer term objectives. This is particularly true if we think the pay-off is longer term, too.

Action – Schedule 15 minutes a day for long term project work such as systems, administration, self-growth or other similar important but non-urgent activities.

Giving a few minutes of attention today to your tomorrow creates over 60 hours a year for key long term results.

LEARNED HELPLESSNESS

Attitude – Imagine the floor your feet are touching right now suddenly gave you an electric shock. You'd move out of there pretty quickly, wouldn't you!?

But what would happen if you couldn't move? What if you had to sit through the shocks?

This was part of the scenario of a series of psychological studies done in the 1960s with dogs. These days, the experiments likely wouldn't pass ethics standards but, at the time, they provided amazing insight into certain behaviors.

At first, the dogs were unable to escape the jolts. Later, they were put in a different room where half the floor was not electrified. Surprisingly, the dogs who were originally exposed to the shocking floor did not move. They just took it. But another set of dogs who had never before felt the jolts quickly moved around to find the safe side of the floor.

So what is the difference?

The first group of dogs had actually learned how to be helpless.

Long story short, psychologists believe that humans are susceptible to this learned helplessness. Along the way, we get into unavoidable negative situations and end up believing that nothing we do will change the situation. To make it worse, we extrapolate that into other scenarios, like work. We learn helplessness because we assume the "entire floor is electrified".

Of course, it is not.

Action - Explore one area where you feel helpless. What have you told yourself about the situation that keeps you stuck? What are you assuming? How have you electrified the whole floor?

_____

Knowing that you only need to move a few feet – in other words, change your perspective or actions, even just a little bit – can give you renewed motivation to make positive changes in your life.

ROLL THE DICE

Attitude – Randomness scares most busy professionals. The idea they could act outside of some routine or habit can be daunting. Yet, part of my own message of success is in advocating randomness.

Parapsychologists study the paranormal – fuzzy unexplained events in the universe. I have my own opinions on it but one interesting thing they have discovered is that people really underestimate coincidence and randomness.

If I flip a coin 10 times and each time it comes up heads, people will bet money on it turning up tails on the next toss. In actual fact, no matter what happened before, there is still only a 50/50 chance it will show up tails. You probably already know this, but you may also forget it at the exact moment of decision-making.

You didn't lose the last business deal or promotion because someone was out to get you. Nor did the traffic lights line up red to spite you when you were already late for that meeting.

Ironically, there is universal order in randomness. Allowing things in your life to happen randomly brings a sense of calm and ease. You are less likely to feel opportunities pass you by because you know that randomness always brings new possibility. There is comfort in occasionally relaxing and allowing things to unfold.

Action – Write down six actions or tasks you could do for the next 30 minutes. Close your eyes and randomly point to one of those actions. Better still, roll a dice and let it randomly pick for you. Then do that action or task.

Notice how you feel, what you think and what you create as a result of allowing randomness to take over for a while.

USING TIME

Attitude - How you use your time reflects how you see yourself. Repeating tasks, creating piles of stuff and generally running around is a clear sign that you do not value your time. If you did, you wouldn't fritter it away through repetition or cluttered confusion.

And when you don't value your time, which is irreplaceable, you don't value yourself, something that is also irreplaceable.

Many of us spend a lot of time looking for new tools to do things better, faster, or cheaper. That is all well and good, but getting things done or creating success is not about techniques.

It is about you.

And none of those fancy ways or nifty gadgets will make one iota of impact until you value yourself.

Action - Across the top of a page, write out this phrase "I value myself by using my time to …." Then fill up the sheet with things you adore doing. The more difficult it is to fill the page, the further down the priority list you may be placing yourself at the moment.

Whether you have filled the sheet with luscious things you are already doing or just want to do, set a goal to dedicate more time doing them. And if you have trouble writing out ways you value yourself, it's time to sit down with a trusted friend and talk this through.

The more you value yourself, the more time you will have to do what you love. It's that simple.

THE POWER HOUR

Attitude – I've said it before and am going to say it again. You cannot manage time. But you can manage the choices you make and the actions you take with the time you have.
And there's a great technique for doing just that!
Have a Power Hour every day.

Action – The Power Hour is used to plan out today, tomorrow, next week, next year or all of them. Use it to review where you are in relation to where you want to be. Spend part of it prioritizing and planning all of today's activities which may include what was missed yesterday.
It's best to have a full Power Hour. You'll find that the 60 minutes of time spent reviewing, planning and strategizing will not only keep you focused and on track but will actually yield several hours of tangible results.

We're often so busy busy busy doing doing doing we forget to ask ourselves if we're actually doing the most effective things!

ON YOUR FEET, MISTER

Attitude – I often get asked for practical advice on how to do things more effectively in the office. One question that keeps coming up is about how to manage meetings, whether scheduled or ad hoc. A big percentage of a professional's day is spent in meetings. And unfortunately, 50% of that time is forever lost!

There are different tips for running highly focused meetings. One of the most valuable is this – for all in-house meetings, have everyone stand up. Unless you're with clients or running a day-long strategic session, get everyone up on their feet for the duration of the meeting.

The results are amazing, as I'm sure you can well imagine. Incidentals are avoided, irrelevant chit-chat is gone and people stay very alert. Over time, pre-meeting preparation is not only done, but becomes much more precise.

I've read several articles on why this type of meeting works so well. Explanations range from "everyone just wants to get back to their own chair" to "a different energy of professionalism and focus is present." It doesn't really matter though, because it works!

So well, in fact, that some newer office designs incorporate this idea into the layout. Conference rooms are often without their traditional board tables or sometimes just include high bar-style tables.

Action – Even if your company doesn't adopt this meeting style, you can. Next time someone walks into your office or cubicle, stand up for the duration of the conversation.

Those who are simply hiding out in your space under the guise of needing information will soon stop and the others will appreciate your focused attention and energy.

Think of it this way – stand up for yourself!

DOING WHAT YOU KNOW

Attitude – People often ask me – "Nancy, why do I not do what I know I need to do?"

Well, the answer is both desperately simple and tortuously complex.

The simple part – because if we have lived our lives or done things in a certain way for so long, the desire to change does not exceed the fear evoked when considering exactly how our lives may become different.

For example, if I suggest to you that one of the best ways to accelerate success is to learn to say "no" to others, your fear of rejection or loss of relationships will put the brakes on any tangible changes in behavior, consciously or not. You know to say "no", but your fear will stop you from doing it.

The complex part – is all in your head. We complicate and worry about the perceived results of changing our behavior or attitude. We create long-winded and muddled scenarios, loaded with images of negative results or feelings. "If I change X, then A, B and C will happen but if they don't, D, E and certainly F will, and I don't like that."

The possible outcomes look both unpredictable and dangerous. This complexity makes it much easier to simply fear the change and therefore do nothing.

Action – Today, make one small alteration in attitude or action that will move you closer to your productivity goals. Have courage and persistence, then notice how easy it is to overcome a fear of change by being conscious to it.

You know what you need to do – now go do it!

HOW WE LEARN SKILLS

Attitude – We all learn work skills in a similar way. Understanding the four stages I'm about to explain means you can realize your power and capacity to learn the skills more easily.

First, we are *unconsciously incompetent*. We don't know what we don't know.

Second, we are *consciously incompetent*. We know we don't know and often feel a bit stupid. We may also tell ourselves that we will always be this way so we don't look to achieve more. This is where we sometimes stop.

Third, we become *consciously competent*. This is when we are starting to learn and incorporate the new skills. It may be slow and some people stop here out of frustration and impatience.

But when we persevere and keep going, we ultimately hit the fourth stage of learning – *unconsciously competent*. We take the actions without really thinking about them.

How you learned to drive a car would be a good example. You go from not really understanding how it all works to thinking you'd never get out of the driveway without hitting something. Then, over time, you get your brain, feet, eyes and hands all working in unison. These days, as you're driving around, you probably have so many unconscious bad habits, you need to go back to driving school!

We all learn skills this way – how to use time effectively, networking, communication, report writing, sales techniques and so on.

(By the way, once you hit the *consciously incompetent* stage, you may want to stop, because "change" is looming. However, you can never go back to being *unconsciously incompetent*. You can never go back to not knowing what you don't know. So, you might as well keep moving all the way through to *unconsciously competent!*)

Action – Which of the four points are you at in one of your productivity skills? What do you need to do to get to the next stage?

_____

Don't give up – keep going through the natural and universal process of learning.

WHAT'S YOUR EXCUSE?

Attitude – The day you *stop* making excuses is the day you *start* making things happen. Each and every excuse you hold on to stops you from creating what you want in work and life!

You are able to be more productive, effective and successful, even if you didn't get your Master's degree, or you had an ogre for a boss, or grew up with little money in your pocket.

When you take full responsibility for yourself, you can create anything.

Action – During the past week, what top three excuses have you used on others or yourself? What can you do, in thought or in action, to remove these excuses from your life?

And by the way, the phrase "I can't do anything because that's just the way I am" is an excuse!

You make things happen, or not, through your thoughts and actions alone. Stop giving that incredible power away to excuses.

OCCAM'S RAZOR

Attitude – Occam's Razor is a 14th century physics principle basically stating that, all things being equal, the simplest option or explanation is the best one. This principle still holds true after almost 700 years as we continue to strive for achievement.

Most of us get drawn into complicated patterns of behavior and we spend tons of money, time and energy looking for an ideal solution. Occam's Razor reminds us that the ideal solution is always in simplicity.

In fact, the solution to many problems is almost always inside of what is currently there.

Action – Instead of searching far and wide for some new-fangled technique or device, what is already within the problem itself that can be tweaked?

What can you simplify right now that would be the foundation of a sustainable solution?

Look for Occam's Razor (simplicity) any time you feel stuck or overwhelmed.

PUSHING PAPER

Attitude – I like to think of myself as an organized person. I generally know where things are and what's on my desk at any given moment. But there is one pile of paperwork that often gets out of control. By what I hear from clients, peers and colleagues, I'm not alone!

It's my stack of reading material.

Articles, papers, books, clippings. You name it, it's there. And I also have a virtual stack of PDFs and bookmarks taking up space on the hard drive, too. All of it often creates a feeling of guilt and overwhelm when I see this pile of unused potential.

I love information and am an advocate of lifelong learning, but it's a fact that we will never know it all. And we don't need to either.

Action – Here are a few tips to help sort out the mass of paper, real and virtual, that clogs up your space and mind.
- There are two types of reading – for work and for pleasure. Never mix the two stacks.
- Always carry reading materials with you. Take advantage of delayed flights or meetings by pulling out articles or clippings while you are waiting.
- Give decided time to reading each week. Whether for work or for fun, reading gives our brains an alternate activity from the "doing doing doing" all the time.
- Limit the size of the stack by using a solid box file or binder to hold it all. Once it's full, purge.
- Limit online storage too. Set a total allowable number by megabytes or documents and stick to it.
- When the next issue of a magazine comes out, online or paper version, throw out the previous issue. It's old news now.

Remember, you don't need to know it all and you certainly don't need to store it all!

TAKING ACTION

Attitude – Success is available to those who understand the simple keys that unlock it. Right now, I want to share with you one of the most important keys to success.

Mark Twain said:

> "Twenty years from now you will be more disappointed by the things you did not do rather than the ones you did do. So throw off your bow lines, sail away from the safe harbor. Catch the trade winds in your sails."

There are a few important points in this quote, but we're only focusing on one. And here it is – take action!

"Geez, I know *that*" I can hear you say. So tell me – how many times have you said recently "Oh, I'll do that tomorrow."

Success isn't about tomorrow. It is available to you right now. Yes, you might be a little afraid or unsure, but don't worry about that.

Action – Take *one* action in the next 30 minutes that will move you closer to getting something done.

As Mark Twain also said – explore, dream, discover.

CONCENTRATION

Attitude – Did you ever play a game called Concentration? Although there are many varieties, the idea is to either match pairs of cards or to name the next item in a category or series. The point is that, to be successful in the game, you need to focus all of your energy to the task at hand. If your mind wanders, you will miss seeing a pair of cards or hearing what the preceding player has said.

Concentration is a skill fundamental to consistent work performance.

Unfortunately, many people tell themselves that they have so much to do, they can't concentrate and focus.

Oh yes you can!

"Okay Nancy, but how can I focus when there are so many demands on my time?"

How to do it is actually the easy part. It's *deciding* to focus – making the choice – that most people won't or don't do. We all know how to turn off the phone, close the door, go somewhere else or hit the "do not disturb" button. However, few people actually give themselves permission to do it, so they stay unfocused and rattled much of the day.

Nothing can create more power in your life and capacity in your day than concentrating your time, energy and resources on a very limited set of targets.

Action – Give yourself permission to use one behavior that will help you concentrate. Pick a method of focus and implement it. Only you can do it.

To attempt to do two things at once is to do neither very well.

WHAT'S 15 MINUTES?

Attitude - Time management is a misnomer. You cannot manage time. An hour is always 60 minutes - no more, no less. But you can manage the choices you make and actions you take with the time you have.

One of the best tips for getting things accomplished is by working in 15 minute chunks for part of the day. However, I find many people resist this idea as they think nothing can really get done in such a small amount of time.

Well, here are some examples of what happens every 15 minutes:
- About 117 babies are born in the USA, and I won't even guess how many are conceived!
- Over 3 billion emails are sent worldwide
- A monarch butterfly on its annual migration will travel about a mile

So, what can you do in 15 minutes? How about -
- answer 5 emails
- plan out your next day's activities
- read a draft proposal
- make one contact call or about 7 voicemail calls
- begin research on that project
- order a gift online for your spouse, colleague or friend
- call your team into your office and say "thank you" for all their efforts
- take a short walk outside

Action - Break a portion of your day into 15 minute chunks and move rapidly through a variety of tasks.

Things don't get done because you spend hours on them. Your accomplishments depend on each individual minute of focused attention.

―――――――――――――――――――――

Every minute really can count!

BANG THE DRUM!

Attitude - Do you like the sound of drums? Or the tambourine? Or maybe the xylophone? All these instruments are percussions, creating rhythms with their sounds.

Guess what? You are creating rhythms too. Yup, every 24 hours, our circadian rhythms create a beat to our own life.

Circadian rhythms are a series of fluctuations from high to low in over 100 of our bodily functions, including body temperature, energy levels, moods, hormone secretions, appetite, sensory acuity and much more. Our ability to learn and perform work tasks is significantly affected by our circadian rhythms.

For example, studies show that alertness drops between 2:00pm to 5:00pm every day for most people. But that's no excuse for slacking off during the afternoon!

What it is, though, is useful information for scheduling your tasks, priorities and events for times when you are most likely to be able to respond effectively to work demands.

Scheduling activities for your "highs" often means being able to work faster, easier, with less effort, and bigger results.

Action - You can learn your individual rhythms by keeping track of your daily fluctuations. It may take a while, perhaps a month of daily tracking, but once you understand your own "beat", you will sleep better at night, have more energy, feel lively, have fewer mood swings and be much more productive.

Take control, and march to your own beat.

HOT POTATO

Attitude – A client recently asked me "Why do people leave me voice messages so late in the day? What could they possibly want from me at 6:00pm?"

My reply is quite simple. "People don't always want *anything* from you at 6:00pm!"

What they often want is to tick another item off their own to-do list. Their message may sound urgent but it's often them wanting to get it off their list that is the urgent part.

Every single professional I know has a mountain of work to do. So that voice message is simply passing responsibility for the next action step on to you. You are the recipient of the proverbial hot potato.

Sometimes people will phone others when they *know* the phone is probably not going to get picked up, simply so they can check it off the list but not have to deal with a "live" person on the other end of the line.

What often happens, though, is that you choose to do something with that hot potato as soon as it is passed to you, at 6:00pm or even later. And immediate action is not always necessary.

Action – Next time someone passes something to you in this way, stop to consider its true urgency. And if it can wait, which it often can, leave it. Do something with it tomorrow.

Let hot potatoes cool down.

FIX THE ROOF

Attitude – The time to fix the roof is not when it's raining but when the sun is shining.

Sure, you're going to have last minute emergencies now and then. But success comes to those who can keep ahead of the present conditions, even just a little bit.

Instead of worrying about what "might" happen, think and plan in advance. Beyond simple contingency plans, I'm referring to being ahead of an approaching situation, both in attitude and in action.

Action – Today, spend an hour thinking and planning ahead on one of your primary projects.
- What are the considerations?
- What elements are coming around the corner but aren't here yet?
- What is happening elsewhere in the marketplace or office environment that has potential to add or subtract from this project?
- Who are key players in the future that need a heads-up now?

Prevention is often better than cure.

IT ALL ADDS UP

Attitude – Being productive, and being successful, is the sum of many small actions that you repeat. Unfortunately, most people take the first step or two, then completely stop.

Productivity and success occur when persistent, consistent action takes place over time. It's not magic or extraordinary. It is not reserved for those with status, money or education. And success certainly isn't about who you know.

It *is* about what you do. And productive people know that what they do generally takes time, patience and focused attention.

Action – Somewhere in your stack of to-do's is something you are avoiding. You're not getting a quick payoff so you continue to avoid any action on it whatsoever.

Well, pull that project out of the pile right now and take the next action. Just the next action. Tomorrow, take another next action. The day after, then another, and so on.

Persistent, consistent action creates success. That's all you need to understand. And it is all you need to do.

I DON'T KNOW HOW

Attitude – The phrase "I don't know how" is a cheap way out. You see, if you are still asking the same how-to question 24 hours later, your inability to find the answer has nothing to do with a lack of knowledge.

It does, however, have everything to do with not having the desire, confidence or courage to find that answer.

These days, any how-to question can be answered within a day. Sometimes, much faster. Using the internet, workplace intranet, numerous education websites, the vast array of instruction manuals, reading a book, and even talking with friends or colleagues, anyone can find the answer to any how-to question.

So what stops you? Well, it could be several things. Maybe you simply don't want to know the answer because it really isn't that important to you. Maybe it's important to someone else, but not you.

Perhaps knowing how to do something will mean you will have to take a next step that feels frightening or unpleasant.

Or maybe you just don't want the responsibility of having the answer to your how-to question. If you know, then you've got to do something with it, right?!

Action – Next time you find yourself stuck for more than a day on a how-to question, ask yourself what is really going on.

Are you nervous about what will happen if you know the answer? Do you want to know? Are you willing to take responsibility for the next step?

A repeated how-to question is a sure sign something else is going on.

HEAVY HAVE-TO

Attitude – The way you define the word "success" will determine how you go about achieving it.

In the early days of my business, my definition centered on the quality and quantity of clients I had, the amount of money in the bank and where I lived. And you know what? It was often an overwhelming struggle to even get close to feeling successful.

Then one day many years ago, I realized I was feeling particularly successful. In fact, I was more motivated, happy and confident than I had been in a long time. I wanted to figure out what was going on.

So I started consciously looking for the patterns and choices I had made that led me to this joyful, calm place. As I looked at my daily schedule, it hit me.

Everything in it – my personal and professional appointments and plans – were all things I *wanted to* be doing. There was nothing in there I *had to* do.

In the weeks preceding, I had been clearing away unwanted activities, just so I could become more focused and productive. I didn't realize that it would actually lead me to be and feel more successful.

By eliminating certain tasks that didn't align with my goals plus changing my perception and attitude toward those that remained, everything became stuff I wanted to do. And not surprisingly, as I continued to focus on doing only those things I wanted to do, the clients, money, and wonderful home all came my way.

Action – Focus all your attention on only those things you *want to* do. Wherever possible, delete or delegate the stuff you *have to* do. For whatever is left, shift your attitude so that you can enjoy the task even if it's not your most favorite thing.

When the heavy have-to's are gone, you will be and feel lighter, brighter and more successful than you thought possible.

IN THE COFFEE SHOP

Attitude – As I write this, I'm sitting in a local coffee shop, armed with a large mug of hot tea, a sweet snack and several pens. However, I am not doing this to avoid work. In fact, I know this departure to a new environment is a way to actually help me get work done.

Like many folks, I'm easily distracted by a ringing phone and incoming emails. Interestingly though, the hustle and bustle of the coffee shop doesn't interrupt my train of thought. I feel motivated and energized. I know this works for me because I've been paying attention to my habits and behaviors – those that support and those that detract.

Action – How else could you execute your to-do's? Is it feasible to spend some time working away from the office? Or perhaps just in another room within the office? How can you remove yourself from noise and distraction to stay focused on the tasks at hand?

Sometimes, physically taking yourself away from distractions is better than trying to grit your teeth through them.

THE FIRST SEVEN MINUTES

Attitude - The first seven minutes of your day can be very important. How we wake from sleep often sets us up for the whole day.

During the night, we pass through several stages of sleep, from a deep sleep to dreaming to a light sleep and back again. Often, though, the cycles of sleep are sharply disrupted by the shrill of the alarm clock. We end up traveling back through the stages very quickly. You'll know this by the confused state you may feel, not knowing what day or time it is when you first open your eyes.

What happens in these first few minutes of being awake can inadvertently affect your mood, decisions, confidence and attitude.

I discovered that my quasi-conscious brain was often filled with negative feedback and information as I sharply awoke. Coming quickly out of dream state, I would hear myself say how rotten the day was going to be, how much work wasn't finished yet and how crappy I felt at my job.

Then I learned how to stop the noise.

Now, I wake up and immediately spend about seven minutes positively reinforcing my attitudes and efforts before even getting out of bed. I talk to myself about how wonderful the morning is and how grateful I am for my life and the adventures ahead in the day. The seven minutes coincide with the snooze bar on my alarm clock.

Action - Tomorrow, no matter how busy your schedule is, use the first seven minutes after the alarm to nip negatives in the bud. Encourage and praise your efforts and have a positive inner conversation.

The first few minutes of the day can significantly impact the whole day. And how it does that is within your conscious control.

EPS

Attitude – In psychology, we are always uncovering really interesting pieces of information to explain why people do what they do. And some of the ways and "reasons" we are unproductive are fascinating!

Tongue-in-cheek, one such strategy for being unproductive is referred to as Empty Project Syndrome. This means people don't complete projects because – oh my goodness – then what would they do with themselves?

And when the project is done, we wouldn't be needed anymore, right? Yes, I did say a person's individual motivators can be interesting. I never said anything about rational.

Yet many professionals, when given an opportunity to be really honest without consequence, often report a fear that shows up just as a project is about to be finished. Instead of feeling complete and accomplished, they are afraid and nervous.

These feelings, which some people call irrational, are simply learned behaviors. Somewhere in our world experience, we have learned that having no big projects to work on means we are not good enough. Or that no one needs our expertise and knowledge.

These same people who suffer from Empty Project Syndrome at work have a hard time with personal projects too. Chaos and half-finished things are everywhere.

If this sounds like you, don't worry. You are not alone. In fact, there are many who feel the same way!

Action - Begin to bust the fears by taking action and completing one outstanding project today.
  Yes, today!
  Then pause for a moment, acknowledge your success and move on to another that can be fully finished within two days.

───────────────────────────────

The more projects you consciously and purposefully finalize within the next four weeks, the less the Empty Project Syndrome will affect your motivation in future.

ME IN THE MIRROR

Attitude – Your outer world corresponds with your inner world. You cannot have a messy desk, filthy car and disorganized schedule while trying to convince others – and yourself – that you are in control and on the path of productivity.

The Law of Correspondence is simple and fundamental. What goes on outside is going on inside.

What is the impression you get of someone who is untidy or all over the place? You probably question their ability to handle your requests or manage your outcomes.

So why then would you expect others to hold you in high regard if your outside world is a mess? What's more, *you* feel the lack of congruence between what you hope to achieve internally and what you are creating externally.

Fortunately, there's no need to navel gaze or dissect your mental processes in order to change this. The Law of Correspondence happens to work in reverse too!

Action – Clean up your desk, tidy the car and organize your schedule. Get rid of any extraneous or useless stuff from the world around you. Fix the broken shelf, rearrange some furniture, and sort out the drawers – whatever is necessary to clear away space.

Maintain an organized external environment and you will find yourself having clarity and calm in your inner world too.

ADDICTED TO LOVE

Attitude – Everyone wants to hear the words "thank you". This is because most of us want to feel we are doing good things for others.

We see their acknowledgement through gratitude in a way that reinforces and encourages us. And that's fine.

But wanting appreciation becomes a problem when it turns into a need for approval from people around us. It is like an addiction when we choose our actions, goals, outcomes and results based on whether or not we think we'll get recognition from others.

This type of behavior is unhealthy and fundamentally destructive.

Maybe you don't think you are an approval seeker. Well, here are some sure signs that your desire for acknowledgement has turned into an addiction:

- You have trouble saying "no" to others.
- You do just about everything the boss or client asks of you, even if it's unreasonable.
- You get annoyed if others do not show you respect or appreciation.
- You choose priorities by the likelihood of gaining respect.
- You do not pursue your dreams because others might mock you.

Whose life is this? Yours or theirs?

Action – The first step in moving beyond the approval addiction is in allowing yourself to do so. Give *yourself* positive reinforcement by celebrating your own accomplishments, without waiting for others to do it for you. Be your own biggest cheerleader.

Sure, receive appreciation with grace. But do not need it.

WORK ISN'T WORK

Attitude - What do you think about the work you do? You see, how you *perceive it* will dictate how you *do it*.

Do you feel dragged down and uninspired on a Monday morning? Do you wonder why you get stuck with boring projects? Have you asked yourself why it has to be so hard?

Or, do you find it exciting to have new opportunities every day, even if you have the same routine? Maybe you feel useful and appreciated simply because you are there. Or perhaps there is an energy of gratitude that fills you as you walk through the door.

I don't work. At all. Ever. And I teach others exactly how to not work, too.

Sure, I used to work. I'd work hard for long hours with little personal or financial reward.

It's only "work" (in its negative connotation) if you'd rather be doing something else.

Would you rather be doing something else right now? Really? What? Why? What would that new career or activity give you that this one doesn't? Are you sure you cannot get that from where you are, even by changing your outlook?

Action - If, after careful review, you decide that what you do is "work", then put a plan into action so you can move to the "something else".

Life is far too short to keep filling it with work!

MOTIVATION IN A MINUTE

Attitude – People frequently ask me "Nancy, how can I stay motivated every day?"

Well, there are a number of psychological theories to explain motivation, like drive theory, self-actualization and so on. But you don't need to know all these.

What you do need to know is the *feeling* of motivation is the culmination of a *thought* process. In a nutshell, the way you interpret a situation, discuss it with yourself and then decide your position, determines whether you are motivated or not.

You can influence that processing and there are many different ways to do that. But instead of looking outside yourself to figure that out, look within.

Action – Start by listing the things you find motivating. It could be money, numbers, reputation, a need to please, fears, pride, your faith, or all of these or others.

Don't worry if what you say is right or wrong for the rest of the world. At this point, simply be honest with yourself. You may choose to evolve them – or not – in future. For now, just acknowledge what exists.

As you come to understand your motivators, you'll be able to leverage them to suit your goals and desired outcomes.

WHAT SEASON ARE YOU IN?

Attitude – No matter where you live in the world, Mother Nature has created seasons. While some regions have spring, summer, fall and winter marked by noticeable changes, others are more mediocre in their differences.

In some parts here in Canada, we can easily go from -40 Celsius in winter to +40C in the summer, with everything in between!

Like the fluctuations of Mother Nature, you too have natural rhythms that affect your productivity and work performance. There are times when we feel strong and positive, able to pursue goals and take risks. At other times, we may be more quiet and sensitive, wanting to relax and just "be" for a while.

Our rhythms may not flow on a calendar like weather does, but do you know your internal signals that tell you it may be time to hibernate for a day or two? Can you sense an upcoming surge of energy? Do you recognize your physical, mental and emotional fluctuations?

Action – Take note of your cycles of energy throughout the week or month. See what patterns emerge for you.

There is no one universal pattern – everyone is very different, particularly over time.

As you come to understand and work with your rhythms instead of forcing against them, you will find yourself feeling more at ease and effective every day.

QUICK SLOW QUICK

Attitude – Wow, things have been hectic recently. And in my business – corporate training, writing, public speaking, consulting – things need to flow with some consistency. Certain times can be slower than others. However, over the last few years, even the slow times seem awfully fast!

This is where I have learned a great lesson. And it's one that has helped me handle huge amounts of activity with very little feeling of overwhelm.

I concentrate on the pace of my work, not the volume of it.

Previously, when I would look around a desk that was covered in tasks and projects, somewhere in the back of my mind, I was counting the things that weren't yet done. As the number climbed, the dread climbed too. I would ask myself "how am I going to manage all these new projects, a bunch of outstanding ones, and all the daily operations of my business?" I would get frustrated and angry.

However, these days I'm focused more on the *pace* of my activities. I can easily choose a fast or slow tempo. Sometimes I work full out for several hours or even days. In the middle of it all, I might slow things down a bit with less activity. Or, vice versa.

I'm not counting how many things are ticked off the list. I'm just maintaining a cadence, whatever I choose that to be. I'm probably ticking off more than ever before, but don't notice it as much. Yet, there is a consistent feeling of achievement and success simply because my primary focus is on pace, not on volume.

Action – For the next five work days, experiment with the pace of your activity rather than the volume. What do you create differently? What becomes easier? More difficult?

When the number of things on the desk feels overwhelming, focus on your pace of activity instead.

NOW YOU SEE IT ...

Attitude – A simple shift of perspective can change everything.

No doubt you have seen one of the many different visual illusions that are out there. If so, you'll know that, whether the illusion is a trick performed by a magician or an image hidden inside another image, just altering the way you look at something alters what you actually see. So, how might changing some of your perspectives change your productivity?

There is no "easy street" or "happily ever after". With that in mind, what if you simply accept that things are supposed to be difficult; that it is actually created and planned that way? What if you realized that part of your role in this life is to be faced with challenges on a regular basis?

Action – Tomorrow, walk into the office *knowing* that some of your day is definitely going to get messed up. Notice how you approach interruptions, disruptions and urgent matters (and the people involved).

What's different? Or the same?

As you accept that challenge is a built-in part of life, you'll worry less about plans falling apart and focus more on just getting things done regardless.

PASS IT ON

Attitude – Does your workday have more work than day? The solution to this problem is quite simple.
Delegate.
Now hold on. Before you turn the page, it is possible for anyone (yes, anyone) to delegate tasks or activities to others. Managers, sales people, admin staff and even home-based sole proprietors can always delegate some of their activities to someone else, even if you have to pay for it yourself.
Kevin, an extremely busy salesman, was overwhelmed by all the admin tasks his manager was now telling him to do. Plus, his client list was larger than before since the team was downsized. It was a constant battle between unpaid admin tasks and those activities that led to financial reward. No matter what he chose, Kevin thought he was losing or missing out on something.
After looking at all his tasks and objectives as well as what he did and didn't like to do, we found about seven hours a week of simple admin and financial activities he could delegate. So he hired a virtual assistant. The money he paid from his own pocket was minimal and the additional high value actions he now had time for more than covered the costs. His exhaustion disappeared and he even started going to his son's after school activities!

Action – Make a list of non-confidential tasks you could have someone else do for you. If you spent as little as $50 a week to hire an assistant of some sort, how much value could you translate that into?

The most productive people delegate. And anyone can do it.

MY DAD

Attitude – My Dad loved starting projects and tasks around the house. I remember a tool box jammed with gadgets and gizmos.

The only problem was that he managed to happily start every project but didn't finish many of them. A half-painted fence and partially finished basement were evidence of his making choices to not follow through.

Most of us start our projects enthusiastically with the intention to get it all done. Well, intention means nothing!

Being productive comes from persistent, consistent actions taken over time. Without the determination to stay the course despite inevitable setbacks, it is likely you will rarely achieve your desired outcomes. Therefore, you will probably be and feel unproductive.

A great way to measure your own levels of persistence is to look around your desk. I'll bet there are several incomplete activities and unfinished projects sitting there. Yes, some may need the input of others and you can't control that, but many may be hanging around because you choose not to take persistent actions.

Action – Be honest. Look right now and evaluate where you are on those incomplete tasks and projects. What actions have you given up on? What needs to happen next? Are you willing to do it? If so, do it. If not, make a decision on what you'll do about it.

Every incomplete project drains your energy.
Persistently move forward or let it go. Just decide!

MULTITASKING

Attitude – It often feels like we're trying to do everything all at once, doesn't it? As it turns out, we are! Well, we're trying to anyway.

With a growing demand (real or perceived) to get things done, workers are trying harder to multitask, or do two or more things at the same time. Some people think multitasking is highly efficient and others believe themselves to be very good at it.

There's only one problem with those assumptions.

Psychologists have repeatedly shown that trying to multitask is actually one of the *least* effective productivity strategies. In fact, our brains do not multitask at all but rather rapidly switch from one thing to another. The more often our brain needs to switch, the longer it takes to do so and the more worn out we feel.

Of course, this won't surprise anyone who tries to talk on the phone while reading an email. Or worse still, typing an email that ends up containing parts of the conversation they are having on the phone!

Action – If you're tired, overwhelmed or feel like nothing is getting done, stop trying to multitask. You're exhausting your cognitive capacity by using up energy switching focus back and forth.

Stay attentive to one thing for as long as needed to complete the task (but no more than 50 minutes at a time). Turn off the phone, set boundaries for others to leave you alone, adjust your email behaviors – whatever it takes.

Multitasking is not a habit for sustained success. In fact, it is quite the opposite.

WATCH IT ... OR NOT

Attitude – Question – What's the first thing many people do when they go on holiday?

Answer – They take off their watch.

When we're away from the office for any extended period of time, we tend to stop clock-watching. We allow pangs of hunger to tell us when to eat. Or we let fatigue lead us to sleep.

Watching the clock adds stress and anxiety to your task-oriented life. Constantly looking at your watch builds a sense of pressure and busyness, completely opposite to the calm and balance you are seeking.

Action – Allow yourself periods of time during the working week when you can remove your watch. Work until you feel hungry or need a break.

Note the feeling of freedom you experience (and you will, with practice). Then, put the watch back on and proceed with the remainder of your regular work day.

Remember: Your watch is a tool, not your master!

WHAT INERTIA REALLY MEANS

Attitude – Inertia is the tendency for an object at rest to remain at rest and an object in motion to remain in motion. Inertia explains why you aren't getting the productivity results you want, despite actually taking action.

You see, another part of the definition often overlooked states that an object will remain in motion at the same rate of speed and in the same direction it's going unless acted upon by a force of some kind. And the object will resist that change to its state of motion.

This means that unless you consciously and purposefully do something different, you will get the same results you're getting now.

Plus, you alone are the force that must create that new action.

Action – What's one thing you could do, starting today, that would make a difference to your productivity? Identify that action and make it happen.

_____

Use the law of inertia to move you forward rather than keep you stuck.

TAKING IT TOO SERIOUSLY

Attitude – Too much seriousness can shorten your life!

Sure, there are important things to do. There are priorities and challenging events. You need to focus energy and resources toward tasks and ambitions. But taking yourself and others too seriously is simply a waste of valuable and precious time.

Look around you right now. How many happy faces do you see? Who has a twinkle in their eye or glow on their face? Probably very few people. It's a shame, really.

We are inundated all day by 24 hour news channels, online real time images and data. We have learned that it's okay to complain without finding solutions. Most threatening of all is the vast quantities of messages we receive through media and other channels that say we just aren't good enough.

All this negative leads to an almost obsessive seriousness. No wonder you sometimes struggle to get things done!

A significant portion of what you spend time worrying about is beyond your control. While you can influence other people and situations, you generally can't change them, so your concerns are not well-placed.

Action – When was the last time you had some fun? I'm not talking about a five minute giggle with a pal. I mean a full day of light-hearted entertainment and relaxation.

Book yourself a day off from all this seriousness. Plan fun activities with friends, family or on your own. Immerse yourself into joy. And then do it again and again.

Life is meant to be enjoyed, not endured.

STOP INTERRUPTING ME

Attitude – Want people to stop interrupting you? Just stick out your tongue.

I'm not kidding!

Think about the last time you saw a child engrossed in play or figuring out a puzzle. Or how about you – maybe when sorting through instructions for your techno toy? Was your tongue peeking through the corner of your mouth a little, grasped tightly by your teeth?

Behavioral scientists call this "tongue showing" and it is a form of non-verbal communication that says "leave me alone".

Through several studies, it has been found that even though it's unconscious to the doer and the observer, this tongue showing behavior sends a message that says "I'm busy and concentrating right now."

You may be giggling about this, but a huge percentage of our face-to-face communication is non-verbal. Tongue showing is done by people of all ages and in a variety of situations who clearly want to send a "do not disturb" message.

Action – Without making full eye contact with someone who looks like they're about to bug you, just put your tongue out a bit near the corner of your mouth. The person may leave you alone or they might pause to reconsider what they are about to ask of you. Or they might offer to help solve what it is you're working on.

Never overdo a technique like this, but this light-hearted non-verbal cue often works.

If Albert Einstein, the Nobel Prize winning physicist and man behind $E = mc^2$, can stick out his tongue (which he is often seen to do in photos), so can you!

DOING YOUR BEST?

Attitude – I felt pretty disappointed yesterday with how little work I got done. At the end of a very busy day, there was still a pile of notes to be sorted, several emails to be answered and an incomplete proposal. And I had started off with such great intentions.

As the work day drew to a close, I even started contemplating bringing some of the tasks home to get ahead of the game.

But then I realized what was going on. That negative voice in my head was playing the "should" game.

"You should have done X instead of Y."

"You shouldn't have squeezed that client call in to such a busy day."

"You should have been far more organized."

"You should be able to handle all this, after all you are a business psychology specialist!"

That voice doesn't show up often anymore, but when she does, man, she packs a punch!

The key to productivity always starts with awareness. And my awareness of the false negative voice led to a new action, and that was to say this: *Doing my best is what I have to offer. Did I do my best today?*

And the answer was a resounding "yes".

Action – Cut yourself some slack by asking that same question. If the true answer is 'no', then you will begin to see your self-sabotaging ways and can change them.

I would imagine that 99% of the time, you are doing your best and that is all anyone, including yourself, can ask for.

GO DEBRIEF YOURSELF!

Attitude – Debriefing your work is important for creating success. Unfortunately, most professionals don't critique their meetings, presentations or interactions and so an excellent opportunity is wasted.

We don't want to because we have only learned to look for what went wrong. Even if you didn't get the deal or influence the other person, what makes it wrong?

Typically, we start our debriefings by looking for negatives. And once we find them, we can't seem to see any positives. No wonder we avoid these types of evaluations!

Whenever I complete any presentation, interview, project or big task, I ask myself only 2 questions:
1. What did I like best about that?
2. What will I do next time?

Notice the first question looks only for positives. And the second doesn't ask "what will I do *differently*", just "what will I do". To presuppose that something needs to be different is to assume something went wrong. Maybe my critique will show that nothing needs to be changed. But if something does, it will come out in the answer more realistically than if I go looking for negatives.

Action – Use this two question debrief for your next five meetings, phone calls, interactions or completed projects. Notice how your reviews actually become a more positive experience.

Evaluating yourself correctly is a key component for creating success and being motivated for consistent and persistent productivity.

YOUR SOURCE OF SUCCESS

Attitude – To achieve the success in life that you want, no matter how you choose to define that, it takes a combination of mindset and skillset. I call it attitude and action.

The actions can be learned. Fortunately, the attitude can be learned too. In fact, almost all beliefs and behaviors associated with productivity are learned. This is great news, because if some of what you already do is not working for you, then you can relearn new attitudes and actions.

Right now, I'm talking about an important attitude that will help you create success. And that's the attitude of having a sense of source.

Some people consider this a spiritual source. Others simply feel grounded and centered when they see their children laugh. Still others will consciously pause to watch the sunset, marvel at the range of colors that sweep the sky after a rainstorm or revel in the scents wafting from a garden.

What do these things really have to do with success? They are all moments when we feel calm, joyful and at peace, even for a few seconds.

The key is to create plans that allow us to go to this personal sense of source frequently. The more often we go there and the longer we stay, the more accomplished we actually feel and then subsequently become.

Action – What is your sense of source? Do you even know what it is?

Write out 5 things that represent a sense of source for you. Whether that is spiritual or not, it doesn't really matter. What is important is that these things create for you an ease, a feeling of balance or warmth in your heart.

_____

What can you do to be with your sense of source today?
Make it happen and then watch what happens.

ARE YOU NUTS?

Attitude – Samuel Beckett once said "some are born mad, some remain so."

What is madness? Why do some people remain mad, as Beckett said? What is his "insanity" all about and how does understanding it help us become more productive and successful. Well, you'll see what I mean as soon as you read this popular definition of insanity:

> *Insanity is going to bed at night wishing things were different and getting up the next day doing exactly the same things.*

Okay, a little tongue-in-cheek about madness, but think about this for a second ... wanting things to be different, but doing nothing about it. That's nuts!

Over and over again, I've heard people talk about wanting to be more productive and focused. Then, they get up the next day and do exactly the same things they did the day before!

One of the first steps in being more productive is to change some of the *things* you are doing, starting right now. Not tomorrow, or next week, or next year.

Right. Now.

The fabulous news is that these *things* can simply be small changes in behavior. They do not have to be huge leaps. (In fact, it is better if they aren't.)

What are some of the things you could change today that will have a positive impact on your tomorrow? Here are a few examples to get you thinking:

- Go to bed 30 minutes earlier so you are getting a good rest.
- Send one card or email per day to a friend, just to say "hi".
- Get up 15 minutes earlier so you aren't rushed in the morning.
- Walk the last mile to or from work for the exercise.
- Tidy up your work area (or any other space) to declutter.
- Spend the first 30 minutes in the office organizing and planning your day.

Action – Make a list of 10 things you would be willing to do in any given day that would positively impact your tomorrow. Commit to implementing at least one every day.

_____

If you don't change something today, you will invariably do exactly the same things as you did yesterday. And if it's not working for you today, it's not going to be working for you tomorrow.

FLIPPIN' EMAIL

Attitude – Research shows that we switch from looking at email to other types of work at least 70 times a day. While that number may seem either high or low to you specifically, it is a stark reminder that mismanaging this particular tool significantly affects our productivity.

You see, the idea of multitasking is a misnomer. Your brain cannot actually do two, high-end thinking functions at the same time. Sure, it can flick back and forth very quickly but there is always a moment of downtime as we switch. Even the brains of young professionals who grew up hooked to computers cannot multitask despite their protests to the contrary!

More importantly, that incessant flipping around is cognitively exhausting. This explains why you might feel tired in the middle of the afternoon. If you've been flipping around email for several hours, your brain is wearing out.

Action – There are no hard and fast rules that work for everyone and their email. Generally, though, limit working on your email to 10 minutes per hour or 30 minutes three times a day. Turn off the tone that signals new emails unless you're expecting something urgent. And do not use email to avoid other tasks on your desk.

Small changes will make a big difference and your brain will thank you for it.

TIPS TO CLEAR THE DESK

Attitude – Most people already know it is important to keep their desk clear, clean and tidy. Yet those same people often tell me they don't know how or they don't have the time.

Well, here is exactly how to have a clearer desk in 30 minutes or less.

Action – First, clear a space where you can create four piles. Next, turn off your phone or ask people to leave you alone for the next 30 minutes.

Then, start at one end of your desk working toward the other end. Everything you touch (other than technology) has to go into one of these four piles:

1. Do
2. Defer
3. Delegate
4. Ditch

The *Do* pile is for those things you must take action on in the next 7-10 days. Do not take the action now, just pile it up.

Defer is for those things that can wait for more than 10 days. Using a sticky note, date the item for when you need to look at it again.

Delegate is the pile for those things that someone else can do. You may not think there is much you can pass to others, but there are generally a few things that end up in this stack.

Of course, *Ditch* is for all those papers that go to recycling, shredding or the garbage.

Be ruthless. Only allow these 4 piles and you will get everything organized in to them.

Then, at the end of 30 minutes, get rid of the *Ditch* stack, date order the *Defer* pile, pass on the *Delegate* batch and sit down to start working in your *Do* stack.

Get yourself organized and I guarantee your day and your week will feel and be more productive and focused without all the stress a messy desk usually brings.

GERONIMO

Attitude – We have memory for many reasons. It helps us to learn, communicate, use logic, create art or connect to a sense of something bigger. It helps us live day to day.

Unfortunately, we have a tendency to remember negative events far more than positive ones. So it takes conscious effort to recall the times in our past that can help us get through our present dilemmas.

I keep photos on my wall of the first day I went skydiving to remind me of just how brave I can be. While work projects, deadlines, events and situations today may *feel* like they'll be the death of me if I fail, none has ever compared to very real fatal possibilities I faced that first day when my parachute did not open properly.

So when I find myself unproductive or overly distracted, I simply look at those photos and remember.

Action – Write a story that includes one or more of your big life challenges. It doesn't have to be a long story. In fact, it could be a simple paragraph. Or, like me, use a series of photos or magazine clippings that demonstrate the story.

Keep the story or photos near. Refer to them whenever you feel yourself wavering with a predicament.

Whatever challenges you may be facing, you have most likely faced them before. The context may be different but the content is similar. And you obviously got through it then, so leverage what you learned now.

WANT MORE DISCIPLINE?

Attitude - Don't spend your time worrying about becoming more disciplined in order to be more productive. I can guarantee you that, right now, you have all the discipline you need. What might be a bit off, though, is where you are directing it.

You put the same amount of discipline into staying stuck as you do to becoming free.

It takes just as much discipline to stay off a healthy eating plan as it does to stay on it.

You are being disciplined in repeating negative behaviors in the same way you would be in repeating positive behaviors.

You see, it is very rare indeed that I meet someone who actually needs *more* of a certain ability. What they need instead is to aim their ability in a different direction, more closely aligned to what they want.

No doubt, a few months or years ago, the direction your ability was pointed was helpful in some way, at that time. But now, at this time, the direction isn't matching the desired outcome anymore.

Action - Draw the four points of a compass on a sheet of paper. Write "discipline" (or whatever word represents the ability you feel you are lacking) where "north" would be located. Place a large dot somewhere else on the compass to represent your current "position" with that ability.

Note your dot is still on the same compass - just pointed in another direction. So, what three things could you do today to redirect your ability toward "north"?

———————————————

Instead of trying to acquire more of a certain ability, start by redirecting the ability you already have. It's there. I guarantee it.

JUST FOCUS ON THREE

Attitude – Feeling overwhelmed by your to-do list? Here is an important technique for reducing the stress and crush that comes with a long list of stuff to do, at work or at home.

Focus on three things at a time.

Your brain doesn't like long lists. Short-term memory can only hold about seven pieces of information. Reduce the length of the list and you will feel lighter and much more motivated.

Of course, the best way to shorten a task list is to stop saying "yes" to everyone and/or just knuckle down and get it all down. But given that it's unlikely either of these will happen in the next 24 hours, here's something you can implement right now. This very minute.

Action – On a piece of paper, write down just three tasks from your longer to-do list that you are prepared to focus on for the next time frame, whether that's an hour, half day, day, week, or whatever. Place your longer list away in a drawer until all three tasks on the shorter list are complete. Then, pull out the longer list and take another three tasks from it, and so on.

Focusing on three activities will give you a sense of confidence in your ability, and a feeling of accomplishment as the items get crossed off. It's fast, simple and very functional.

GETTING ORGANIZED

Attitude – Panic often follows disorganization.
 I frequently get calls and emails from people who feel overwhelmed and desperate. They are racing, and often simultaneously back-peddling, complaining there's not enough time, support or fairness in this corporate world.
 And they're right. So, their choice then becomes to (a) do something about it or (b) continue with the pity party.
 Generally, I go for (a).

Action – First, understand that you cannot actually manage time, so it becomes about choice and action management instead.
 The most fundamental way to get a grip on your choice and action management is to devote time each day to get organized. To categorize papers and projects. To sort out your mind and thoughts.
 Even before you begin to plan your next steps, take no less than 15 minutes a day to put your internal and external spaces in order.

Getting into the simple habit of organizing your space will quickly reap huge financial, emotional, physical and psychological rewards for you.

WITHOUT A DOUBT

Attitude - People question why it is they aren't as productive as they want to be. For many, the answer is simple.
Doubt.
When we doubt our ability to do something or our capacity to handle the consequences, we will hit the brakes and go nowhere. Our doubts can turn a straightforward task into a complicated mess. We will hum and haw, waste time and avoid tasks based on one tiny little thought.
Doubt.
A thought of doubt leads to a belief of inability. That belief turns into a fear which prevents any action from being taken. No action means no result, other than getting nothing done.
The philosopher Thomas Carlyle said, "Doubt, of whatever kind, can be ended by action alone." You see, once actions are taken, the fears subside, ability is apparent and doubt diminishes.

Action - So, what is one action you will take today on just one task that has been causing fear?

Identify and take action, without doubt.

ITTY BITTY BITS OF TIME

Attitude – There are always little chunks of time in the day that feel a bit wasted, like when you're waiting for a return phone call or a meeting to start, hanging around in a client's office, riding in the taxi or simply standing around.

Those chunks don't feel long enough to get started on anything, so we often just twiddle our thumbs or play games on some phone app.

While I'm definitely an advocate of using five minutes here or 10 minutes there to quietly rest and regroup or to visualize or meditate, there are other ways to use those short gaps, too.

Action – First, always have some low-priority work or reading with you that you can grab when there's dead time.

Second, make lists of what you can do with five, 10 and 15 minutes. For example, in five minutes, I can file papers or tidy my workspace. In 10 minutes, I can make a phone call or review my to-do list. And in 15 minutes, I can complete a step in a larger project or organize my email inbox, even from my cellphone.

And finally, use short amounts of time to connect with others. Ask your colleagues how they are, phone your spouse simply to say hello, or write a quick "thank you" note to one of the many people who undoubtedly deserve your gratitude.

The time may be "itty" but there's lots of
"bits" that can be done with it.

28 DAYS MORE?

Attitude – How often do you pick up a sheet of paper, glance at what needs to be done and then drop it back down into the pile again?

I'll bet you'll do exactly the same thing the next day, too.

Research into our work habits show that almost all of us touch each of our work tasks more than once. In fact, it's estimated that we spend the equivalent of 28 days each year just pushing our work around the desk. No wonder we feel overwhelmed with things to do!

Just imagine how much clearer and in control your work space would be if you cut this habit in half. And just imagine what you could accomplish with those extra days.

You could get a big project started *and* finished, you could take a vacation, you could spend many hours with friends and family – the list is endless.

Action – Today, commit to touching three pieces of work just once. Pick it up, complete it and move on. Do the same tomorrow.

There is a lot you could do with 28 "extra" days a year. Start today!

I LIKE WORK ...

Attitude – A smile came to my face the other day as I read the words of humorist Jerome K. Jerome. He said, "I like work. It fascinates me. I can sit and look at it for hours."

Some days are just like that, hence my knowing smile.

It is difficult sometimes to find the focus, energy, or motivation to do the work. At times, we procrastinate because we don't know what to do next. Or because the task is unpleasant or, in our own mind, unrelated or irrelevant to us. But sometimes, it really doesn't matter what the reason is for our procrastination.

Sometimes it is best simply to honor it.

Yes, you heard me – honor it.

But, with that honoring must also come a resolution of commitment. So, for me, instead of sitting and looking at it for hours, I may give myself permission to sit for just one hour.

And sure enough, if the resolution is strong, the work gets done after that hour has passed.

Action – So, today, when you notice your procrastination, let it be what it is for a while (up to an hour). Don't overanalyze or overthink.

Then, when the time you've allotted is done, follow up on your commitment and get that work done. Or figure out the problem underneath the procrastination.

Sometimes, it's okay to let things sit. For an hour.

PLAYING CATCH UP?

Attitude - You cannot manage time, only the choices you make and actions you take with the time you have. And one of the most important choices you can make is to not get caught up in the game of catch-up!

Work-life balance research shows that most professionals spend upwards of 70% of their day doing tasks that are either unproductive or take them away from their job priorities.

So, if you are one of those who frequently says "I don't have time", you have jumped into a pattern of catch-up behavior. You get distracted and pulled in various directions far too easily.

But you already know this, don't you?!

What's important now is deciding what you're going to do about it.

Action - Track your time in 30 minute chunks for three weeks. Go through each day and total up how much time you choose to spend in three different categories:
- Wasted time
- Urgent tasks
- Priorities

Commit to managing each of these three categories. Start by choosing to eliminate wasted time. Next, understand that most urgent tasks come from non-urgent stuff that is ignored or mismanaged by you or someone else. These tasks or projects must be systematized. Finally, your priorities are those that are scheduled first and directly relate to your performance goals. Choose to spend at least 50% more time in this category of activity each day.

Schedule your priorities and make them happen. Make it your choice.

DON'T MICROMANAGE

Attitude – What is your plan of action for today?
Please note – I'm not asking what's on your to-do list or what you'd like to get done. I want to know what your *plan* is.

If you cannot answer that question, you may find yourself getting to the end of your workday wondering what happened.

Here was mine for today:
8:00am - check and manage emails
9:00am – 30 minute client call
10:30am - project A
11:30am - manage emails
1:00pm - 15 minute client call
2:30pm - writing project
5:00pm - final email check and leave for home

Notice I'm not micromanaging my schedule. Not every single minute is accounted for. Only my top priorities are listed. All other tasks and interruptions fit around these.

This plan moves projects forward, allows flexibility and accommodates my personal desire for spontaneity, all while giving me structure and measures.

Action – There is no one-size-fits all when it comes to planning. So, arrange your day to focus on certain priorities while allowing for the inevitable distractions and fiddly bits that are a part of your specific personality and job requirements.

Winston Churchill wasn't kidding when he said
"he who fails to plan is planning to fail."

DISH UP THE BRAIN FOOD

Attitude – How do you feed your brain?

I'm talking about more than just salmon, broccoli, or apples. Brain food is also what you expose it to – your brain always responds to the mental nutrition you give it as well as the physical.

If you give you brain too much routine, it *will* be bored. So throw it a curve occasionally. Use your computer mouse with your left hand instead of your right, or vice versa. Purposefully change your morning routine every few days. Drive on different roads to get to work or try a new recreational activity.

If you want to focus on the positive things around you, then hang out with positive people, stay away from the news and read inspiring books. If you constantly fill your brain with negatives, then it will focus on negatives.

Action – Do one thing differently today. And laugh 10% more often.

Yes, you are what you eat. But you're also what you think about.

WANT MORE?

If you would like even more access to the daily *Simple Sound Solutions* audio program, sign up at:

www.nancymorris.com/solutions

SELECTED BIBLIOGRAPHY

Aiello, J.R., & Shao, Y. (1993). Electronic performance monitoring and stress: The role of feedback and goal setting. In M. J. Smith & G. Salvendy (Eds.) *Human-Computer Interaction: Application and Case Studies* (pp. 1011-1016). Amsterdam: Elsevier Science

Al Kalaldeh, M.T., & Abu Shosha, G. M. (2012). Application of the perceived stress scale in health care studies – An analysis of literature. *International Journal of Academic Research, Part B, 4(4)*, 45-50

Ariely, D. (2012). *The (honest) truth about dishonesty: How we lie to everyone- -especially ourselves.* Harper Collins.

Avey, J. B., Luthans, F., Smith, R. M., & Palmer, N. F. (2010). Impact of positive psychological capital on employee well-being over time. *Journal of Occupational Health Psychology, 15*(1), 17-28. doi:10.1037/a0016998

Baker, D.G., Nash, W.P., Litz, B.T., Geyer, M.A., Risbrough, V.B., Nievergelt, C.M., Webb-Murphy, J. A. (2012). Predictors of risk and resilience for posttraumatic stress disorder among ground combat marines: Methods of the marine resiliency study. *Preventing Chronic Disease, 2012(9)*. doi: 10.5888/pcd9.110134

Bakker, A.B. (2009). Building engagement in the workplace. In R. J. Burke & C.L. Cooper (Eds.), *The peak performing organization* (pp. 50-72). Oxon, UK: Routledge

Bakker, A. B., & Daniels, K. (2013). *A Day in the Life of a Happy Worker*. New York, NY: Psychology Press.

Bakker, A. B., & Xanthopoulou, D. (2009). The crossover of daily work engagement: Test of an actor–partner interdependence model. *Journal of Applied Psychology*, 94(6), 1562-1571. doi:10.1037/a0017525

Bandura, A. (1986). *Social foundations of thought and action: A social cognitive theory*. Englewood Cliffs, NJ: Prentice-Hall.

Barker, R. G. (1963). The stream of behavior as an empirical problem. In R. G. Barker (Ed.), *The stream of behavior*, (pp. 1-22). New York, NY: Appleton-Century-Crofts

Baron, R. A., Hmieleski, K. M., & Henry, R. A. (2012). Entrepreneurs' dispositional positive affect: The potential benefits – and potential costs – of being "up". *Journal of Business Venturing*, 27(3), 320-324. doi:10.1016/j.jbusvent.2011.04.002

Bauer, J. J. & Perciful, M. S. (2009). Constructivism. In S. Lopez (Ed.). *Encyclopedia of positive psychology*. Malden, MA: Wiley-Blackwell.

Baumeister, R. F., Bratslavsky, E., Muraven, M., & Tice, D. M. (1998). Ego depletion: Is the active self a limited resource? *Journal of Personality and Social Psychology*, 74, 1252-1265

Baumeister, R.F., Stillwell, A.M., & Heatherton, T.F. (1995). Personal narratives about guilt: Role in action control and interpersonal relationships. *Basic and Applied Social Psychology*, 17, 173-198. doi: 10.1080/01973533.1995.9646138

Baumeister, R. F., Bratslavsky, E., Finkenauer, C., & Vohs, K. D. (2001). Bad is stronger than good. *Review of General Psychology*, 5(4), 323-370. doi:10.1037//1089-2680.5.4.323

Beal, D. J., & Weiss, H. M. (2013). The episodic structure of life at work. In A. B. Bakker & K. Daniels (Eds.) *A Day in the Life of a Happy Worker*. London: UK: Psychology Press

Beal, D. J., Weiss, H. M., Barros, E. & MacDermid, S. M. (2005). An episodic process model of affective influences on performance. *Journal of Applied Psychology, 90,* 1054-1086.

Beck, A. T. (1979). *Cognitive therapy and the emotional disorders.* New York, NY: Meridian

Bennett, S. (2014). *Get it done: From procrastination to creative genius in 15 minutes a day.* New World Library.

Biggs, J. B., & Moore, P. J. (1993). *The process of learning.* New York, NY: Prentice-Hall.

Bjornholt, M., & Farstad, G. R. (2012). 'Am I rambling?' on the advantages of interviewing couples together. *Qualitative Research, 14*(1), 3-19. doi:10.1177/1468794112459671

Boster, J. (2005). Emotion categories across languages. In H. Cohen & C. Lefebvre (Eds) *Handbook of categorization of cognitive science.* (pp. 187-222) Amsterdam: Elsevier.

Branden, N. (1994). *The six pillars of self-esteem.* New York, NY: Bantam.

Brooks, A. (2014). Get excited: reappraising pre-performance anxiety as excitement. *Journal of Experimental Psychology: General, 143*(3), 1144-1158. doi:10.1037/a0035325

Brothers, W. C. (2005). *Language and the pursuit of happiness: A new foundation for designing your life, your relationships & your results.* Naples, FL: New Possibilities Press.

Bstan-'dzin-rgya-mtsho, & Cutler, H. C. (1998). *The art of happiness: A handbook for living.* New York, NY: Riverhead Books.

Buckingham, M., & Coffman, C. (1999). *First, break all the rules: What the world's greatest managers do differently.* New York, NY: Simon & Schuster.

Burton, C. M., & King, L. A. (2004). The health benefits of writing about intensely positive experiences. *Journal of Research in Personality, 38*(2), 150-163. doi:10.1016/S0092-6566(03)00058-8

Cabrera, D. (2011). How to think (video). TEDx Talks. Retrieved from https://www.youtube.com/watch?v=dUqRTWCdXt4

Cameron, J. (1992). *The artist's way: A spiritual path to higher creativity.* Self-published.

Canfield, J., & Switzer, J. (2005). *The success principles: How to get from where you are to where you want to be.* New York, NY: Harper Resource Book.

Carbonara, S. (2013). *Manager's Guide to Employee Engagement.* New York, NY: McGraw-Hill.

Carr, A. (2011). *Positive psychology: The science of happiness and human strengths* (2nd Ed.). London, UK: Routledge

Carver, C.S., Scheier, M.F., & Weintraub, J.K. (1989). Assessing coping strategies: A theoretically based approach. *Journal of Personality and Social Psychology, 56(2),* 267-283. doi: *10.1037/0022-3514.56.2.267*

Catford, L. R., & Ray, M. L. (1991). *The path of the everyday hero: Drawing on the power of myth for solving life's most important challenges.* Los Angeles, CA: J.P. Tarcher.

Chang, E.C., & Sanna, L.J. (2003). Optimism, accumulated life stress, and psychological and physical adjustment: Is it always adaptive to expect the best. *Journal of Social and Clinical Psychology: 22(1),* 97-115. doi: 10.1521/jscp.22.1.97.22767

Chang, E. C., Asakawa, K., & Sanna, L. J. (2001). Cultural variations in optimistic and pessimistic bias: Do easterners really expect the worst and westerners really expect the best when predicting future life events? *Journal of Personality and Social Psychology, 81*(3), 476-491. doi:10.1037/0022-3514.81.3.476

Charvet, S. R. (1997). *Words that change minds: Mastering the language of influence.* Dubuque, IA: Kendall/Hunt Pub. Co.

Cialdini, R. B. (2007). *Influence: The psychology of persuasion.* New York: Collins.

Cohen, S., & Janicki-Deverts, D. (2012). Who's stressed? Distributions of psychological stress in the United States in probability samples from 1983, 2006 and 2009. *Journal of Applied Social Psychology, 42,* 1320-1334. doi:10.1111/j.1559-1816.2012.00900.x

Cohen, S., Kamarck, T., & Mermelstein, R. (1983). A global measure of perceived stress. *Journal of Health and Social Behavior, 24,* 385-396.

Cohen, S., & Williamson, G. (1988). Perceived stress in a probability sample of the United States. In S. Spacapan & S. Oskamp (Eds.), *The social psychology of health.* (pp. 31-67) Thousand Oaks, CA: Sage Publications

Conyers, M., & Wilson, D. (2015). *Positively smarter: Science and strategies for increasing happiness, achievement, and well-being.* Oxford, UK: Wiley Blackwell

Covey, S. R. (1989). *The seven habits of highly effective people: Restoring the character ethic.* New York: Simon and Schuster.

Crandall, B., Klein, G. A., & Hoffman, R. R. (2006). *Working minds: A practitioner's guide to cognitive task analysis.* Cambridge, MA: MIT Press.

Cross, J. (2007). *Informal learning: Rediscovering the natural pathways that inspire innovation and performance.* San Francisco, CA: Pfeiffer/Wiley.

Csikszentmihalyi, M. (1993). *The evolving self: A psychology for the third millennium.* New York, NY: HarperCollins Publishers.

Csikszentmihalyi, M. (1999). If we are so rich, why aren't we happy? *American Psychologist, 54*(10), 821-827. doi:10.1037//0003-066X.54.10.821

Dagenais-Desmarais, V., & Savoie, A. (2011). What is psychological well-being, really? A grassroots approach from the organizational sciences. *Journal of Happiness Studies, 13*(4), 659-684. doi:10.1007/s10902-011-9285-3

Davidson, R. J., & Begley, S. (2012). *The emotional life of your brain: How its unique patterns affect the way you think, feel, and live--and how you can change them.* New York, NY: Hudson Street Press.

de Jong, T., Wiezer, N., de Weerd, M., Nielsen, K., Mattila-Holappa, P., & Mockallo, Z. (2016). The impact of restructuring on employee well-being: A systematic review of longitudinal studies. *Work & Stress: An International Journal of Work, Health & Organizations, 30(1)*, 91-114. doi:10.1080/02678373.2015.1136710

Diener, E., Suh, E., Lucas, R., & Smith, H. (1999). Subjective well-being: Three decades of progress. *Psychological Bulletin, 125(2)*, 276-302. doi:10.1037/0033-2909.125.2.276

Diener, E. (1984). Subjective well-being. *Psychological Bulletin, 95*(3), 542-575. doi:10.1037/0033-2909.95.3.542

Diener, E., & Diener, C. (1996). Most people are happy. *Psychological Science, 7*(3), 181-185. doi:10.1111/j.1467-9280.1996.tb00354.x

Dweck, C. S. (2006). *Mindset: The new psychology of success.* New York, NY: Random House.

Dworkin, R. W. (2006). *Artificial happiness: The dark side of the new happy class.* New York, NY: Carroll & Graf.

Dyer, W. W. (1976). *Your erroneous zones.* New York, NY: Funk & Wagnalls.

Ekman, P. (1999). Basic emotions. In T. Dalgleish & M. Power (Eds) *Handbook of Cognition and Emotion.* (pp 45-60). Sussex, UK: John Wiley & Sons. Retrieved from https://www.paulekman.com/wp-content/uploads/2013/07/Basic-Emotions.pdf

Emmons, R. A., & McCullough, M. E. (2003). Counting blessings versus burdens: An experimental investigation of gratitude and subjective well-being in daily life. *Journal of Personality and Social Psychology, 84*(2), 377-389. doi:10.1037//0022-3514.84.2.377

Feuerstein, R., & Lewin-Benham, A. (2012). *What learning looks like: Mediated learning in theory and practice, K-6.* New York, NY: Teachers College Press.

Feuerstein, R., Feuerstein, R. S., & Falik, L. H. (2010). *Beyond smarter: Mediated learning and the brain's capacity for change.* New York: Teachers College Press.

Fisher, P., & Wells, A. (2009). *Metacognitive therapy: Distinctive features.* London, UK: Routledge.

Fleming, S. M. (2014). The power of reflection: Insight into our own thoughts, or metacognition, is key to higher achievement in all domains. *Scientific American Mind, 25*(5), 30-37. doi:10.1038/scientificamericanmind0914-30

Fleming, S. M., & Lau, H. C. (2014). How to measure metacognition. *Frontiers in Human Neuroscience, 8.* doi:10.3389/fnhum.2014.00443

Folkman, S. (1997). Positive psychological states and coping with severe stress. *Social Science Medicine, 45*(8), 1207-1221. doi:10.1016/S0277-9536(97)00040-3

Folkman, S. (2008). The case for positive emotions in the stress process. *Anxiety, Stress & Coping, 21*(1), 3-14. doi: 10.1080/10615800701740457

Folkman, S., & Moskovitz, J. T. (2000). Positive affect and the other side of coping. *American Psychologist, 55*(6), 647-654. doi:10.1037/0003-066X.55.6.647

Ford, B., & Mauss, I. (2014). The paradoxical effects of pursuing positive emotion – When and why wanting to feel happy backfires. In J. Gruber & J. T. Moskowitz (Eds) *Positive emotion: Integrating the light sides and dark sides* (pp. 363-381). Oxford: Oxford University Press.

Fordyce, M. W. (1977). Development of a program to increase personal happiness. *Journal of Counseling Psychology, 24*(6), 511-521. doi:10.1037/0022-0167.24.6.511

Forgas, J. P., & East, R. (2008). On being happy and gullible: Mood effects on skepticism and the detection of deception. *Journal of Experimental Social Psychology, 44*, 1,362-1,367. doi:10.1016/j.jesp.2008.04.010

Frederickson, B. L. (2009). Positive emotions. In C. S. Snyder & S. J. Lopez (Eds). *Oxford handbook of positive psychology.* (pp. 120-134) Oxford: Oxford University Press.

Fredrickson, B. L. (1998). What good are positive emotions? *Review of General Psychology, 2(3),* 300-319. doi:10.1037/1089-2680.2.3.300

Fredrickson, B. L. (2001). The role of positive emotions in positive psychology: The broaden-and-build theory of positive emotions. *American Psychologist 56(3), 218-226.* doi:10.1037/0003-066X.56.3.218

Fredrickson, B. L. (2009). *Positivity.* New York, NY: Crown Publishers.

Fredrickson, B. L., & Joiner, T. (2002). Positive emotions trigger upward spirals toward emotional well-being. *Psychological Science, 13*(2), 172-175. doi:10.1111/1467-9280.00431

Friedman, R. (2014). *The best place to work: The art and science of creating an extraordinary workplace.* New York, NY: TarcherPerigee.

Frijda, N. H. (1993). Moods, emotion episodes, and emotions. In M. Lewis & J. M. Haviland (Eds.), *Handbook of emotions* (pp. 381-403) New York, NY: Guildford Press

Fullagar, C., & Kelloway, E. K. (2013) Work-related flow. In A. B. Bakker & K. Daniels (Eds.) *A day in the life of a happy worker.* (pp. 41-57) New York, NY: Psychology Press

Gander, F., Proyer, R. T., Ruch, W., & Wyss, T. (2012). Strength-based positive interventions: Further evidence for their potential in enhancing well-being and alleviating depression. *Journal of Happiness Studies, 14,* 1241-1259. doi:10.1007/s10902-012-9380-0

Garcia, D., Garas, A., & Schweitzer, F. (2012). Positive words carry less information than negative words. *EPJ Data Science, 1*(3), 1-12. doi:10.1140/epjds3

Gilbert, D. T. (2006). *Stumbling on happiness*. New York, NY: A.A. Knopf.

Gladwell, M. (2005). *Blink: The power of thinking without thinking*. New York, NY: Little, Brown and Co.

Gottlieb, B.H. (Ed.) (1997). *Coping with chronic stress*. New York, NY: Plenum Press

Grant, A. M., Christianson, M. K., & Price, R. H. (2007). Happiness, health or relationships: Managerial practices and employee well-being tradeoffs. *Academy of Management Perspectives*, 51-63. doi:10.5465/AMP_2007_2642123

Griffeth, R. W., Hom, P. W., & Gaertner, S. (2000). A meta-analysis of antecedents and correlates of employee turnover: Update, moderator tests, and research implications for the next millennium. *Journal of Management, 26*(3), 463-488. doi:10.1177/014920630002600305

Griffiths, B., & Kaday, C. (2004). *Grow Your Own Carrot: Motivate Yourself to Success!* London, England: Hodder & Stoughton.

Gruber, J., Kogan, A., Quoidbach, J., & Mauss, I. B. (2013). Happiness is best kept stable: Positive emotion variability is associated with poorer psychological health. *Emotion, 13(1)*, 1-6. doi:10.1037/a0030262

Gruber, J., Mauss, I. B., & Tamir, M. (2011). A dark side of happiness? How, when, and why happiness is not always good. *Perspectives on Psychological Science, 6(3)*, 222-233. doi:10.1177/1745691611406927

Halpern, D. F. (1996). *Thinking critically about critical thinking*. Mahwah, NJ: L. Erlbaum Associates.

Hart, K. E., & Sasso, T. (2011). Mapping the contours of contemporary positive psychology. *Canadian Psychology-psychologie Canadienne, 52*(2), 82-92. doi:10.1037/a0023118

Hazelton, S. (2013). *Great days at work: How positive psychology can transform your working life*. London, England: Kogan Page Limited.

Hefferon, K., & Boniwell, I. (2011). *Positive psychology: Theory, research and applications*. Maidenhead, Berkshire: McGraw Hill Open University Press.

Hejazi, A., & Salarifar, M. (1999). Analyzing the effectiveness of metacognitive components on academic achievement. *Journal of Massage of Counselor, 3,* 124-132

Held, B. S. (2004). The negative side of positive psychology. *Journal of Humanistic Psychology, 44(9)*, 9-46. doi:10.1177/0022167803259645

Hershfield, H. E., Scheibe, S., Sims, T. L., & Carstensen, L. L. (2013) When feeling bad can be good: Mixed emotions benefit physical health across adulthood. *Social Psychology Personal Science, 4(1),* 54-61. doi:10.1177/1948550612444616

Hill, N. (2015). *The law of success: The 21st century edition*. High Roads Media.

Hulsheger, U. R. & Schewe, A. F. (2011). On the costs and benefits of emotional labor: A meta-analysis of three decades of research. *Journal of Occupational Health Psychology, 16(3),* 361-389, doi:10.1037/a0022876 Retrieved from http://www.lib.sun.ac.za/Library/eng/finding/CPDWell%282012%29/Hulsheger.pdf

In Bakker, A. B., & In Leiter, M. P. (2010). *Work engagement: A handbook of essential theory and research*. Hove, England: Psychology Press.

Jaipal-Jamani, K. (2014) Assessing the validity of discourse analysis: transdisciplinary convergence. *Cultural Studies of Science Education, 1(7)*. doi:10.1007/s11422-013-9567-7

James, W. (1884). What is an emotion? *Mind, 9(34),* 188-205. doi: 10.1093/mind/os-IX.34.188 Retrieved from http://psychclassics.yorku.ca/James/emotion.htm

Jellison, J. M. (2006). *Managing the dynamics of change: The fastest path to creating an engaged and productive workforce*. New York, NY: McGraw-Hill.

Joyner, M., & Recorded Books, Inc. (2007). *The irresistible offer: How to sell your product or service in 3 seconds or less*. Prince Frederick, MD: Recorded Books.

Kanner, A. D., Coyne, J. C., Schaefer, C., & Lazarus, R. S. (1981). Comparison of two modes of stress measurement: Daily hassles and uplifts versus major life events. *Journal of behavioral medicine*, 4(1), 1-39.

Kashdan, T., & Biswas-Diener, R. (2014). *The upside of your dark side: Why being your whole self--not just your "good" self--drives success and fulfillment*. New York, NY: Hudson Street Press.

Katie, B., & Mitchell, S. (2002). *Loving what is: Four questions that can change your life*. New York, NY: Harmony Books.

Kauffman, C., & Silberman, J. (2009). Finding and fostering the positive in relationships: positive interventions in couples therapy. *Journal of Clinical Psychology*, 65(5), 520-531. doi: 10.1002/jclp.20594

Kent, M., In Davis, M. C., & In Reich, J. W. (2014). *The resilience handbook: Approaches to stress and trauma*.

Keyes, C. L., Shmotkin, D., & Ryff, C. D. (2002). Optimizing well-being: The empirical encounter of two traditions. *Journal of Personality and Social Psychology*, 82(6), 1007-1022. doi:10.1037/0022-3514.82.6.1007

Kiely, S., & Sevastos, P. (2008). Emotional labour: A significant interpersonal stressor. *InPsych: The Bulletin of the Australian Psychological Society Ltd, 30(2)*, 16-17.

Klaff, O. (2011). *Pitch anything: An innovative method for presenting, persuading and winning the deal*. New York: McGraw-Hill.

Kruger, J., & Dunning, D. (1999). Unskilled and unaware of it: How difficulties in recognizing one's own incompetence lead to inflated self-assessments. *Journal of Personality and Social Psychology*, 77(6), 1121-1134. doi:10.1037/0022-3514.77.6.1121

Laszlo, J., Cserto, I., Fulop, E., Ferenczhalmy, R., Hargitai, R., Lendvai, P., Peley, B., Polya, T., Szalai, K., Vincze, O. & Ehmann, B. (2013) Narrative language as an expression of individual and group identity: The narrative categorical content analysis. *SAGE Open, 3*, 1-12. doi:10.1177/2158244013492084

Layous, K., & Lyubomirsky, S. (2012). The how, why, what, when, and who of happiness: Mechanisms underlying the success of positive interventions. In J. Gruber & J. Moscowitz (Eds.). *The Light and Dark Side of Positive Emotions*. New York, NY: Oxford University Press.

Lazarus, R. S. (2003). Does the positive psychology movement have legs? *Psychological Inquiry, 14(2)*, 93-109. doi:10.1207/S15327965PLI1402_02

Lazarus, R. S., & Folkman, S. (1984). *Stress, appraisal, and coping*. New York: Springer Pub. Co.

Levinson, D. J. (1985). *The seasons of a man's life*. New York, NY: Knopf

Lindebaum, D., & Fielden, S. (2011). 'It's good to be angry': Enacting anger in construction project management to achieve perceived leader effectiveness. *Human Relations, 64*, 437-458. doi:10.1177/0018726710381149

Linley, P. A., Joseph, S., Maltby, J., Harrington, S., & Wood. (2009). Positive psychology applications. In S. J. Lopez & C. R. Snyder (Eds.) *The Oxford handbook of positive psychology (2nd ed)*. (pp. 35-47). New York, N.Y.: Oxford University Press

Livingston, J. A. (1997). *Metacognition: An overview*. Retrieved from http://gse.buffalo.edu/fas/shuell/cep564/metacog.htm

Loehr, J. E. (2007). *The power of story: Rewrite your destiny in business and in life*. New York, NY: Free Press.

Lomas, T., Hefferon, K., & Ivtzan, I. (2014). *Applied positive psychology: Integrated positive practice*. London: Sage

Lunsford, A. A., & Ruszkiewicz, J. J. (1999). *Everything's an argument.* Boston, MA: Bedford/St. Martin's.

Luthans, F. (2002). The need for and meaning of positive organizational behavior. *Journal of Organizational Behavior, 23*(6), 695-706. doi:10.1002/job.165

Lyubomirsky, S., & Della Porta, M. D. (2010). Boosting happiness, buttressing resilience: Results from cognitive and behavioral interventions. In J. W. Reich, A. J. Zautra, & J. Hall (Eds.), *Handbook of adult resilience: Concepts, methods, and applications.* (pp. 450-464). New York: Guilford Press. Retrieved from http://sonjalyubomirsky.com/wp-content/themes/sonjalyubomirsky/papers/LDinpressb.pdf

Lyubomirsky, S., Sheldon, K.M., & Schkade, D. (2005). Pursuing happiness: The architecture of sustainable change. *Review of General Psychology, 9(2),* 111-131. doi:10.1037/1089-2680.9.2.111

Lyubomirsky, S., & Layous, K. (2013). How do simple positive activities increase well-being? *Current Directions in Psychological Science, 22*(1), 57-62. doi:10.1177/0963721412469809

Lyubomirsky, S., King, L., & Diener, E. (2005). The benefits of frequent positive affect: Does happiness lead to success? *Psychological Bulletin. 131,* 803-855 doi:10.1037/0033-2909.131.6.803

Mauss, I. B., Savino, N. S., Anderson, C. L., Weisbuch, M., Tamir, M, & Laudenslager, M. L. (2012) The pursuit of happiness can be lonely. *Emotion,* 12(5), 908-912, doi:10.1037/a0025299

Mauss, I. B., Tamir, M., Anderson, C. L., & Savino, N. S. (2011). Can seeking happiness make people unhappy? Paradoxical effects of valuing happiness. *Emotion, 11,* 807-815. doi:10.1037/a0022010

McGuire-Snieckus, R. (2014) Hope, optimism and delusion. *The Psychiatric Bulletin, 38(2),* 49-51. doi:10.1192/pb.bp.113.044438

McKelvey, C. (2013). *Stanford 2013 Roundtable panelists demystify the secrets of happiness*. Retrieved from http://news.stanford.edu/news/2013/october/roundtable-happiness-science-101813.html

Mendoza, A. (n.d.). *Happiness psychology and biology: Happiness research shows what happens to the brain when we are happy*. Retrieved November 16, 2014 from http://allie8020.hubpages.com/hub/Happiness-Psychology-and-Biology-Happiness-Research-Shows-What-Happens-to-the-Brain-When-We-Are-Happy

Mentis, M. T., Dunn-Bernstein, M. J., & Mentis, M. (2008). *Mediated learning: Teaching, tasks, and tools to unlock cognitive potential*. Thousand Oaks, CA: Corwin Press

Meyers, M. C., Van Woerkom, M., & Bakker, A. B. (2013). The added value of the positive: A literature review of positive psychology interventions in organizations. *European Journal of Work and Organizational Psychology, 22*(5), 618-632. doi:10.1080/1359432x.2012.694689

Miller, J. B. (1986). *Toward a new psychology of women*. Boston: Beacon Press.

Moore, M. T., & Fresco, D. M., (2012). Depressive realism: A meta-analytic review. *Clinical Psychology Review, 32,* 496-509

Morris, N. (2016). *Metacognitive skills training as a positive psychology intervention for within-person fluctuations of wellbeing at work* presented to University of East London, London, England.

Munby, H., Versnel, J., Hutchinson, N. L., Chin, P., & Berg, D. H. (2003). Workplace learning and the metacognitive functions of routines. *Journal of Workplace Learning, 15*(3), 94-104. doi:10.1108/13665620310468432

Muraven, M., & Baumeister, R. F. (2000). Self-regulation and depletion of limited resources: Does self-control resemble a muscle? *Psychological Bulletin, 126*(2), 247-259. doi:10.1037/0033-2909.126.2.247

Murray, B. (2002). *Writing to heal: By helping people manage and learn from negative experiences, writing strengthens their immune systems as well as their minds.* Retrieved from http://www.apa.org/monitor/jun02/writing.aspx

Narragon, K., & Watson, D. (2009) Positive affectivity. In S. Lopez (Ed.). *Encyclopedia of positive psychology.* (pp. 707-711). Malden, MA: Wiley-Blackwell.

Nelson, T. O., & Narens, L. (1990). Metamemory: a theoretical framework and new findings. In G. H. Bower (Ed.) *The psychology of learning and motivation, Vol 26*: 125-173. San Diego, CA: Academic Press

Niederhoffer, K. G., & Pennebaker, J. W. (2009) Sharing one's story – On the benefits of writing or talking about emotional experience. In C. R. Snyder & S. J. Lopez (Eds). *Oxford handbook of positive psychology.* (pp. 573-583) Oxford: Oxford University Press.

Norem, J. K., & Illingworth, K. S. (1993). Strategy-dependent effects of reflecting on self and tasks: Some implications of optimism and defensive pessimism. *Journal of Personality and Social Psychology, 65*(4), 822-835. doi:10.1037//0022-3514.65.4.822

Normann, N., Van Emmerik, A. A., & Morina, N. (2014). The efficacy of metacognitive therapy for anxiety and depression: A meta-analytic review. *Depression and Anxiety, 31*(5), 402-411. doi:10.1002/da.22273

Novak, J. D., & Gowin, D. B. (1984). *Learning how to learn.* Cambridge, England: Cambridge University Press.

Oettingen, G. & Gollwitzer, P. M. (2010). Strategies of setting and implementing goals. In J. E. Maddux & J. P. Tangney (Eds), Social psychological foundations of clinical psychology. (pp. 114-135). New York: The Guildford Press

Oettingen, G. (2014). *Rethinking positive thinking: Inside the new science of motivation.* New York: Penguin

Oishi, S., & Kurtz, J. (2011). The positive psychology of positive emotions: An avuncular view. In K. Sheldon, T. B. Kashdan & M. F. Steger (Eds.), *Designing Positive Psychology: Taking Stock and Moving Forward*. New York: Oxford University Press. doi:10.1093/acprof:oso/9780195373585.003.0007

Packard, D. (1995). *The HP way: How Bill Hewlett and I built our company*. New York, NY: Harper

Peale, N. V. (1952) *The power of positive thinking*. New York: Prentice-Hall

Peters, T. J., & Waterman, R. H. (1982). *In search of excellence: Lessons from America's best-run companies*. New York, NY: Harper & Row.

Peterson, C. (2006). *A primer in positive psychology*. Oxford: Oxford University Press.

Peterson, C., & Seligman, M. E. (2004). *Character strengths and virtues: A handbook and classification*. Washington, DC: American Psychological Association.

Pinker, S. (1997). *How the mind works*. New York, NY: Norton.

Pinker, S. (2002). *The blank slate: The modern denial of human nature*. New York, NY: Viking.

Pinker, S. (2007). *The stuff of thought: Language as a window into human nature*. New York, NY: Viking.

Pratto, F., & John, O. P. (1991). Automatic vigilance: The attention-grabbing power of negative social information. *Journal of Personality and Social Psychology, 61*(3), 380-391. doi:10.1037/0022-3514.61.3.380

Pruyne, E. (2011). Corporate investment in employee wellbeing – the emerging strategic imperative. Retrieved from http://www.nuffieldhealth.com/corporate-wellbeing

Rath, T., & Harter, J. K. (2010). *Wellbeing: The five essential elements*. New York, NY: Gallup Press

Reason, J. (1990). *Human Error*. Cambridge: Cambridge University Press

Robbins, J. (2012). *Nine minutes on Monday: The quick and easy way to turn managers into leaders*. New York, NY: McGraw-Hill.

Robison, J. (2010, June 9). The business case for wellbeing. Retrieved from http://www.gallup.com/businessjournal/139373/business-case-wellbeing.aspx

Rogers, C. R. (1980). *A way of being*. Boston, MA: Houghton Mifflin.

Ryan, R. M., & Deci, E. L. (2001). On happiness and human potentials: A review of research on hedonic and eudaimonic well-being. *Annual Review of Psychology*, 52(1), 141-166. doi:10.1146/annurev.psych.52.1.141

Ryff, C. D. (1989). Happiness is everything, or is it? Explorations on the meaning of psychological well-being. *Journal of Personality and Social Psychology*, 57(6), 1069-1081. doi:10.1037/0022-3514.57.6.1069

Ryff, C. D. (1995). Psychological well-being in adult life. *Current Directions in Psychological Science*, 4(4), 99-104. doi:10.1111/1467-8721.ep10772395

Sarbin, T. R. (1986). *Narrative psychology: The storied nature of human conduct*. New York: Praeger.

Scherer, K. R. (2005). What are emotions? And how can they be measured? *Social Science Information Sur Les Sciences Sociales*, 44(4), 695-729. doi:10.1177/0539018405058216

Schooler, J.W., Ariely, D., & Loewenstein, G. (2003). The pursuit and assessment of happiness can be self-defeating. In I. Brocas and J. Carrillo (Eds.) *Psychology and Economics*, Vol 1, (pp. 41-70). Oxford: Oxford University Press

Schraw, G. (1998). Promoting general metacognitive awareness. *Instructional Science*, 26(1), 113-125. doi:10.1023/A:1003044231033

Schueller, S. M. (2012). Creating a recommendation framework for positive psychology exercises: The Netflix model of positive psychology. *Dissertation Abstracts International: Section B: The Sciences and Engineering, 73(3-B)*.

Retrieved from http://repository.upenn.edu/cgi/viewcontent.cgi?article=1491&context=edissertations

Schunk, D. H. (2008). Metacognition, self-regulation, and self-regulated learning: Research recommendations. *Educational Psychology Review, 20*(4), 463-467. doi:10.1007/s10648-008-9086-3

Schwarz, N., & Strack, F. (2004). How to think (and not to think) about your life: Some lessons from social judgement research. In S. Neiman (Ed.) *Zum Gluck* (pp. 163-182). Berlin, Germany: Akademie Verlag. Retrieved from http://sitemaker.umich.edu/norbert.schwarz/files/schwarz_strack_happiness_einstein-ch_2004.pdf

Scollon, C.N., & King, L.A. (2004). Is the good life the easy life? *Social Indicators Research, 68*(2), 127-162. doi:10.1023/B:SOCI.0000025590.44950.d1

Scott, S. (2002). *Fierce conversations: Achieving success at work & in life, one conversation at a time.* New York, NY: Viking.

Seligman, M. E. (2002). *Authentic happiness: Using the new positive psychology to realize your potential for lasting fulfillment.* New York: Free Press.

Seligman, M. E. (2011). *Flourish: A visionary new understanding of happiness and well-being.* New York: Free Press.

Sell, A., Tooby, J., & Cosmides, L. (2009). Formidability and the logic of human anger. *PNAS, 106*(35), 15073-15078. doi:10.1073/pnas.0904312106

Shapiro, S. L., Oman, D., Thoresen, C. E., Plante, T. G., & Flinders, T. (2008). Cultivating mindfulness: effects on well-being. *Journal of Clinical Psychology, 64*(7), 840-862. doi:10.1002/jclp.20491

Sheldon, K. M., & Lyubomirsky, S. (2006). How to increase and sustain positive emotion: The effects of expressing gratitude and visualizing best possible selves. *The Journal of Positive Psychology, 1*, 73-82. doi:10.1080/17439760500510676

Shrier, B. (1986). *Let's think for a minute.* Goderich, Canada: Signal Books.

Sinek, S. (2009). *Start with why: How great leaders inspire everyone to take action.* New York, NY: Portfolio.

Smith, M. & Segal, J. (2015). *Laughter is the best medicine: The health benefits of humor and laughter.* Retrieved from http://www.helpguide.org/articles/emotional-health/laughter-is-the-best-medicine.htm

Smyth, J. M. (1998). Written emotional expression: Effect sizes, outcome types, and moderating variables. *Journal of Consulting and Clinical Psychology, 66(1),* 174-184. doi: 10.1037/0022-006X.66.1.174

Spender, D. (1980). *Man made language.* London, England: Routledge & Kegan Paul.

Sweeny, K. & Shepperd, J.A. (2010). The costs of optimism and the benefits of pessimism. *Emotion, 10(5),* 750-753. doi:10.1037/a0019016

Tamir, M. (2009). What do people want to feel and why? Pleasure and utility in emotion regulation. *Current Directions in Psychological Science, 18(2),* 101-105. doi:10.1111/j.1467-8721.2009.01617.x

Tarricone, P. (2011). *The taxonomy of metacognition.* New York, NY: Psychology Press.

Tavris, C. (1982). *Anger, the misunderstood emotion.* New York: Simon and Schuster.

Taylor, J. B. (2008). *My stroke of insight: A brain scientist's personal journey.* New York, NY: Viking.

Tracy, B. (2000). *The 100 absolutely unbreakable laws of business success.* San Francisco, CA: Berrett-Koehler.

Tracy, B. (2002). *Focal point: A proven system to simplify your life, double your productivity, and achieve all your goals.* New York, NY: Amacom.

Uchida, Y., & Kitayama, S. (2009). Happiness and Unhappiness in East and West: Themes and Variations. *Emotion, 9(4),* 441-456. doi:10.1037/a0015634

Ury, W. (2007). *The power of a positive No: How to say No and still get to Yes*. New York, NY: Bantam Books.

Vacharkulksemsuk, T., & Fredrickson, B. (2013) Looking back and glimpsing forward: The broaden-and-build theory of positive emotions as applied to organizations. In A. B. Bakker (Ed) *Advances in Positive Organizational Psychology, Volume 1*, (pp.45-60) UK: Emerald Group Publishing Limited

Waterman, A. (2013). The humanistic psychology-positive psychology divide: Contrasts in Philosophical Foundations. *American Psychologist, 68*(3), 124-133. doi:10.1037/a0032168

Wegener, D.T., & Petty, R.E. (1994). Mood management across affective states: The hedonic contingency hypothesis. *Journal of Personality and Social Psychology, 66(6)*, 1034-1048. doi: 10.1037/0022-3514.66.6.1034

Whitmore, J. (2009). *Coaching for performance: GROWing human potential and purpose : the principles and practice of coaching and leadership*. Boston, MA: Nicholas Brealey.

Wieth, M. B., & Zacks, R. T. (2011). Time of day effects on problem solving: When the non-optimal is optimal. *Thinking & Reasoning, 17*(4), 387-401. doi:10.10 80/13546783.2011.625663

Wilson, J. L., & Wright, J. V. (2006). *Adrenal fatigue: The 21st century stress syndrome: What it is and how you can recover your energy, immune resistance, vitality and enjoyment of life*. Petaluma: Smart Publications.

Witters, D., & Agrawal, S. (2015, October 27). Well-being enhances benefits of employee engagement. Retrieved from http://www.gallup.com/businessjournal/186386/enhances-benefits-employee-engagement.aspx

Wood, J. V., Perunovic, E. W. Q., & Lee, J. W. (2009). Positive self-statements - Power for some, peril for others. *Psychological Science, 20*(7), 860-866. doi:10.1111/j.1467-9280.2009.02370.x

Wright, T. A., & Cropanzano, R. (2004). The role of psychological well-being in job performance. *Organizational Dynamics, 33*(4), 338-351. doi:10.1016/j.orgdyn.2004.09.002

Xanthopoulou, D., & Bakker, A. B. (2013). State work engagement: The significance of within-person fluctuations. In A. B. Bakker & K. Daniels (Eds.) *A day in the life of a happy worker.* (pp. 25-40) New York, NY: Psychology Press

Xanthopoulou, D., Bakker, A. B., & Ilies, R. (2012). Everyday working life: Explaining within-person fluctuations in employee well-being. *Human Relations, 65*(9), 1051-1069. doi:10.1177/0018726712451283

Zacks, J. M., Tversky, B., & Iyer, G. (2001). Perceiving, remembering, and communicating structure in events. *Journal of Experimental Psychology: General, 130*(1), 29-58. doi:10.1037/0096-3445.130.1.29

Zimmerman, B. J. (1986). Becoming a self-regulated learner: Which are the key subprocesses? *Contemporary Educational Psychology, 11*(4), 307-313. doi:10.1016/0361-476x(86)90027-5

END NOTE

While enjoying this book, you may have noticed a couple of interesting things about the chapters in Section 2. Specifically, some of the chapters have similar themes, although they are told with different stories. Furthermore, several chapters appear to contradict others. These two things address a few important points woven throughout this entire volume.

First, in order to effectively rethink your "time management" attitudes and actions, it is important to revisit them several times. Reading something once, or even twice, may have absolutely no impact whatsoever. Sometimes, it takes numerous readings to create an action or a change in thought process. Already known in the advertising world, it can take several exposures to a message before you consciously recognize that it is even there, let alone consider making a purchase (or, in this case, a change in attitude and action).

Second, it is important to challenge your thinking by creating opposite positions, not only to what you already think but to what you are learning from this book. This dialectic approach of thesis, antithesis and synthesis improves learning, implementation and retention. It can also validate what you already hold to be true for you.

Third, by improving your experience with the material via the two points above, you are more likely to share the ideas with others. The best way to learn is to teach, so I take steps to encourage that process. Plus, there is no greater compliment to an author than to have a reader share their learning with friends, family or colleagues. To be perfectly honest, even if you don't agree with what I've suggested in a particular chapter, or the entire book for that matter, your debating the point with someone creates exponential growth opportunities for all who discuss it.

The depth of your self-awareness equals the breadth of your success, however you choose to define it. This is particularly true when it comes to being aware of the choices you make and the actions you take at work. It is not possible to "rethink" anything, including "time management", unless you have insight into what you're thinking in the first place. By repeated exposure to an idea, by dialectic engagement with your own thinking, and through talking with other people, you are deepening your self-awareness and breadth of success.

ABOUT THE AUTHOR

In her innovative and internationally-acclaimed audio program, *Simple Sound Solutions*, Nancy Morris reshapes how the business world works around us by showing us how to rethink the business world within us. Now, in her signature book series, *The Morris Code*™, Nancy simplifies even further what others often make so complex.

A "pracademic" (an academic practitioner), Nancy has been studying, researching and writing about the science of business psychology, mindset and motivation for over 25 years. She is a pioneer in the emerging science of using metacognitive self-awareness to create consistent work performance. Nancy is also a specialist in the educational approaches of microlearning, using small pieces of information to create big learning impact.

Called the "un-guru" by her clients, Nancy's no-nonsense approach to translating academic theories into actionable insight for the real world has made her a sought-after speaker and consultant to corporate, small business and individual clients worldwide.

Nancy lives in Ottawa, Canada, is married, has two stepchildren, a cat and a penchant for chocolate-covered almonds!

Contact Nancy through www.NancyMorris.com

CPSIA information can be obtained
at www.ICGtesting.com
Printed in the USA
LVOW13s2150180117
521455LV00001B/1/P